Inspiring Trust does a first-rate job of providing practical insights on effective leadership through a focus on trust: what it is, how some people develop it, how to spot it in yourself and in others.

—William G. Ouchi, PhD, Sanford and Betty Sigoloff Distinguished Chair in Corporate Renewal, UCLA Anderson School of Management, author of the *New York Times* bestseller, *Theory Z: How American Management Can Meet the Japanese Challenge*

Clinton McLemore offers practical insights on how trust—and with it leadership—is earned everyday in our workplaces and in our relationships. As he recommends, "mark it up and make it yours."

—Charles P. Ries, Former U.S. Ambassador to Greece; currently Vice President, International, The RAND Corporation

The strategies outlined by Dr. McLemore will challenge leaders at every level to move beyond natural ability and intellect, toward trustworthy, effective leadership.

—Jeff S. Barney, Vice President & General Manager, Toshiba America

We've recently implemented many of Clinton's strategies. *Inspiring Trust* deftly gives organizations a fresh approach to dynamic leadership in an increasingly competitive marketplace.

—Warren I. Mitchell, Chairman of the Board, Clean Energy

A profoundly meaningful work on the art, science, and practice of leadership. It's succinct but comprehensive, and intelligent yet eminently accessible . . . useful to both aspiring leaders and organizations seeking to identify and develop leaders.

—G. Joyce Rowland, SVP, Human Resources, Diversity and Inclusion, Sempra Energy

Dr. McLemore's wonderful book gives us a blueprint on exactly how to build organizations of the highest trust, greatest impact and most meaningful outcomes.

—R. J. Kelly, Founder and Chief Visionary Officer, Wealth Legacy Family of Companies

Trust is a journey and not a destination. This is a great roadmap!

—Dennis V. Arriola, CEO, Southern California Gas Company

Inspiring Trust is easy to read and full of real-world examples and how-to-do-it tips . . . provides great insight into how to develop and maintain trust in people below, above, and beside you.

—Brigadier General (CA) Emory J. Hagan, III,
Director, Safety and Enforcement Division,
California Public Utilities Commission

Bravo to Clinton McLemore! Whether you're a young aspiring manager or a veteran of the business world, this book offers practical strategies to improve your effectiveness as a leader.

—Jeffrey W. Martin, CEO of San Diego Gas & Electric

A gold mine. Filled with real-life examples, *Inspiring Trust* helps you turn strategy into practice, and reflects the wisdom gained from decades of helping leaders succeed. Owning this book is like having an executive coach with you at all times.

—Michael H. Misumi, Chief Information Officer (CIO),
Johns Hopkins Applied Physics Laboratory

Dr. McLemore's keen intellect, intuitive thinking, and decades of experience combine to make him the best person I know to write about trust and leadership. I would especially recommend this book to young professionals.

—Willis B. Wood, Jr., Former CEO of
Pacific Enterprises; Past Chairman of the Automobile
Association of America (AAA); Member, Board of
Trustees, University of Southern California

This book will prove invaluable to leaders and prospective leaders in fields ranging from business, academia, government and the non-profit sector.

—Malcolm Gillis, University Professor, Rice University

It's rare to find a book that so effectively captures and breaks down the components of leadership. Dr. McLemore analyzes situational dynamics with stories that can add value to anyone's career.

—Betsy Berkhemer-Credaire, Co-owner of Berkhemer
Clayton Retained Executive Search, author of
*The Board Game: How Smart Women
Become Corporate Directors*

A timely and significant topic for leaders. I *like* the two axes of trust: competence and character.

—J. Kenneth Thompson, Owner and CEO,
Pacific Star Energy, LLC; Member of
the Board of Directors of Alaska Air Group,
Pioneer Natural Resources, Coeur Mining, Inc., and
Tetra Tech, Inc.; Former Executive Vice President of ARCO

Having navigated my way up the corporate latter for decades, the trip would have been a lot easier if I had read this book early on. Use it as an ongoing resource.

—Carl Anderson, President of the Board of Directors,
Kaweah Delta Health Care District

Inspiring Trust

Strategies for
Effective Leadership

Clinton W. McLemore

 PRAEGER

AN IMPRINT OF ABC-CLIO, LLC
Santa Barbara, California • Denver, Colorado • Oxford, England

Library of Congress Cataloging-in-Publication Data

McLemore, Clinton W., 1946–
   Inspiring trust : strategies for effective leadership / Clinton W. McLemore.
     pages cm
   Includes bibliographical references and index.
   ISBN 978-1-4408-3357-1 (hard copy : alk. paper) — ISBN 978-1-4408-3358-8 (ebook)
1. Leadership.   I. Title.
   HD57.7.M39583   2014
   658.4'092—dc23   2014017831

ISBN: 978-1-4408-3357-1
EISBN: 978-1-4408-3358-8

18 17 16 15 14   1 2 3 4 5

This book is also available on the World Wide Web as an eBook.
Visit www.abc-clio.com for details.

Praeger
An Imprint of ABC-CLIO, LLC

ABC-CLIO, LLC
130 Cremona Drive, P.O. Box 1911
Santa Barbara, California 93116-1911

This book is printed on acid-free paper ∞

Manufactured in the United States of America

To Major Kevin J. Stepp (USMC)

Contents

To the Reader

Both the *Wall Street Journal* and *Harvard Business Review* have highlighted declining trust as a major contributor to adverse social conditions, both political and economic. Trust in the leaders of organizations—whether large or small, profit or nonprofit, government or private—is increasingly important, perhaps because it seems to be in decline. It is often the missing link in leadership.

This book is for any executive, officer, director, manager, or supervisor who wants to become a better leader. It will help you move those you intend to lead from surface compliance to genuine alignment—internalization of your vision, mission, and goals.

Let me add that if you do not align with those above you, it will be difficult to persuade them of your noble intentions, or to get them to accept your good ideas or constructive feedback. It may also prove challenging to get subordinates to do what you say, but not what you do.

Leadership is enrolling and enfranchising others, and in a democratic society this only occurs when they trust your competence and character. *Inspiring Trust* demonstrates *how* to foster this trust by engaging in specific behaviors that prompt those around you—supervisors, peers, subordinates—to develop confidence in your capability and credibility, to conclude that you (a) know what you're doing and (b) will look out for their welfare and the good of the enterprise.

In the past decade, there has been growing interest in trust. Several books on the topic have already appeared. None of them, however, offers the practical advice captured in the pages that follow. Books about trust typically focus more on the *what* than the *how.* They offer discussions about the importance of trust, but mostly high-altitude generalities on how actually to facilitate it. *Inspiring Trust,* by contrast, offers concrete counsel on what to do to enhance trust—and what not to do. You will note, for example, how everything you say, even at a company social event, is on the record. And, you will see why it makes no sense to pay unnecessary social prices.

Here are some of the other issues addressed in the book: why it's wise to monitor how often you talk in meetings, and how rambling erodes trust; that it's important not to appear rattled by bad news, and why it's necessary to be predictable; how it's usually better to ask, "What's in it for the organization?" than "What's in it for me?"; why others need to *see* your commitment to results, as well as your self-insight and self-restraint; how to engender trust during a conversation by making the other person feel special, as if he or she were the only other person on the planet—showing that you sincerely care; ways to ask for feedback that provide actionable information rather than flattery or reassurance; why expressing empathy is important; how to persuade others to make sacrifices they might not otherwise make, since work involves toil; and, why persuasion grounded in trust is absolutely essential to leadership.

THE CENTRALITY OF ETHICS

Throughout this book, you will find references to the importance of integrity. One of the two central ideas around which it has been crafted, in fact, is trust in your character.

Without integrity, you will never be an effective leader. You may be able to get others to go along with your wishes, perhaps by threatening them, but unless they perceive you as honorable, they will never become true followers. If you obtain only superficial compliance, they will go their own way as soon as they are out of sight, if for no other reason than to prove, if only to themselves, that they are unwilling to be coerced. To lead others, they have to vote for you with their hearts. You have to move them from compliance to alignment.

A good leader is one who fosters loyalty and commitment, and inspires others to do what they might never have thought possible. Within any free society, where members of organizations have at least some choice regarding how much effort to put forth, you cannot be an effective leader without demonstrating honorability. This can be faked only for a while. Sooner or later, its absence becomes apparent, and when it does, compliance and alignment begin sharply to diverge. If your subordinates conclude you are ethically challenged, they may tend to stop asking what's good for the organization and start focusing primarily on what's best for them.

From time to time, a certain amount of pain, suffering, and sacrifice is required of people for an organization to thrive. To think otherwise is naïve. What's good for the enterprise is not always convenient or comfortable. And when it's not, people must be willing to subordinate their wishes and preferences, within reason, to the overall good. They have to be willing to pay personal prices. Such prices can be as much mental as physical. Those within the organization have to think often and intently about its welfare, to devote their creative energies to figuring out how to make it better. Others will do this *only* if they see you doing it also.

HOW TO USE THIS BOOK

When I coach executives and managers, I advise them to use *Inspiring Trust* as both a textbook and a field manual. Because it contains a large number of principles you can actually apply, it is worthy of serious study—or so, at least, many people have told me. Unlike the typical textbook, however, there are no problems to solve at the end of each chapter. Think of it as a guidebook you can keep in your desk and refer to when needed.

Mark it up and make it your own. Such diligence will be rewarded.

CWM

Acknowledgments

A writer is fortunate to have even one friend who is willing to read and comment on a manuscript. I am more than fortunate in having several, each of whom went through all or part of the final draft for this book with a sharp editorial eye. These include Bill Wood, retired CEO of a large publicly traded company; Terry Fleskes, former CFO for its two major subsidiaries; Melissa Rowe, a vice president for what I and others consider to be the nation's preeminent think tank; Mark Pocino, an executive who later became a managing director of a national consulting firm; Ed Fong, a multitalented mathematician; Mark Sweeney, a keen-minded strategic analyst; Carl Anderson, chairman of the board for a large regional health network; Jack Hagan, a brigadier general; and Malcolm Gillis, former president of Rice University. The talented Elizabeth Esser also made helpful suggestions. My eminently literate daughter, Anna-Marie, read through the manuscript several times, offering insightful line-by-line edits.

During the past three decades, I have been able to work with and for a broad array of companies, led by executives from whom I have learned much. Many of the concepts I picked up early on from Warren Mitchell, for example, echo through these pages.

Duncan Merritt encouraged me to write this book. He contributed pivotally to the structure of an address on trust and leadership I first delivered several years ago. It was Duncan's fine suggestion that I organize it around the two axes of competence and character. That talk, which I was invited to give by Jessie Knight, then CEO of San Diego Gas & Electric, ultimately became the book's conceptual skeleton.

My wife, Anna, continues to bring me joy and happiness. She was the first to urge me to write *Inspiring Trust*. Over the years, I've learned a great deal from her about leadership simply by watching. I continue to marvel at how naturally and smoothly she is able to work with people to bring out the best in them.

Hilary Claggett, my highly competent editor at Praeger, has been admirably responsive and routinely helpful.

Finally, I express appreciation for Anne Devlin of the Max Gartenberg Literary Agency. She is uncommonly conscientious, impeccably ethical, and always encouraging. Thank you, Anne!

ONE

The Centrality of Trust to Leadership

For almost thirty years, I've worked as an organizational psychologist. Earlier, I'd been a practicing clinician with full-time academic appointments: six years at a liberal arts college, followed by nine years on the faculty of a doctoral program where I was heavily involved in training psychologists.

A major reason for changing careers from clinical to organizational psychology was my growing interest in leadership. I'll describe in the following pages what sparked this interest and my study of the relationship between leadership and trust, but first, I want to share two misconceptions I once had about people who run organizations. That was before I knew much about how organizations actually work.

TWO MISUNDERSTANDINGS

First, perhaps from characters I saw on TV, I'd developed the impression that people who lead organizations spend their afternoons playing golf. This is almost never the case, and those national economies in which managing directors routinely left for their clubs in the early afternoon did not fare well. It takes commitment, stamina, and resilience to run an organization, whether commercial or nonprofit. Successful leaders work hard, and the faint of heart need not apply for their jobs.

Second, I had developed the idea that management didn't necessarily require a high level of intelligence. Perhaps this was because those few business majors I met in college didn't seem especially gifted. But I was wrong again. The vast majority of people who lead organizations of any size are impressively keen-minded. Almost all of them can digest large amounts of information quickly—and tell you what it means. The capacity to process information is a key component of intelligence.

Before Hunt-Wesson was acquired by Con-Agra and moved to Nebraska, I consulted a day a week at their corporate headquarters in California. At the time, it was the largest producer of tomato products in the world. I believe its CEO, Al Crosson, had only completed high school. But Norton Simon, who owned the company, had the good sense to appoint him national sales manager at the age of twenty-six. By the time Crosson became Hunt-Wesson's CEO, he knew precisely how many palettes of Wesson Oil, Hunt's Tomato Sauce, Paste, and Ketchup, Orville Redenbacher Popcorn, Peter Pan Peanut Butter, La Choy Asian food, and Rosarita beans came out of their factories, and where they were going. He understood the subtleties of market penetration as few executives did.

A THIRD MISUNDERSTANDING

A basic equation in my discipline is $P = A \times M$ (Performance = Ability × Motivation), and so before I had much corporate experience I assumed that, when a leader failed, it was probably because of a lack of one or both. Important as they are, ability and motivation by themselves are rarely sufficient for long-term success; as I will try to show, a number of other qualities are necessary, and without them, the probability of underperformance or outright failure goes up markedly. In reality, few leaders fail because they are insufficiently gifted or inadequately motivated.

You can be extraordinarily intelligent and relentlessly driven without capturing the hearts and minds of those who work for you. And, if you don't capture their hearts and minds, they may well leave your organization. Sooner or later, there will be a brain drain. It may not be apparent for a while, but your inability to win them to your cause—whatever that happens to be—will eventually catch up with you. Unless we're talking about a great deal of it, money alone—compensation and benefits— provides little or no protection against resignations and departures, certainly by the most talented, who always remain a flight risk. Because the enterprise down the street can often outbid you, something more has to hold your highly valued human assets.

A few abusive geniuses have been able to retain their employees because these employees realized that their leader was so creatively gifted that, if they stuck around, they would probably be able to retire at the age of thirty-five or forty. But, such instances are rare.

It used to be the case that people worked in one organization for most, if not all, of their lives. This is no longer true, and it is commonplace for someone to change companies every seven to ten years. I still do psychological assessments of executive candidates, and I can assure you that résumés today look different than they did even a decade ago. When I see a résumé that shows only one employer, especially if there's no history of increasing responsibility, I find myself wondering if there's something wrong. When I first started consulting, however, I would be more skeptical if the résumé didn't reflect stable long-term employment.

Many people, particularly the more talented ones, will not stay with a company unless they perceive certain qualities in their leaders. Even if they do stay, they will rarely contribute everything they could unless their leaders have demonstrated these traits and thereby engendered their loyalty. Instead of getting out of bed at 3:00 A.M. to jot down an innovative idea, they'll roll over and go back to sleep. By morning, the idea may be lost.

WHAT I LEARNED FROM GALLUP

Although its change in ownership was not much publicized, the Gallup Organization was acquired in 1988 by Selection Research, Inc., which had been founded decades earlier by psychologist Donald Clifton. He and I both belonged to the same small professional organization, so I got to know him.

He repeatedly emphasized that, from among Gallup's vast array of survey items, the one that best predicts a wide range of positive organizational outcomes is something along the lines of, "Someone at work cares about me." That's not the whole story behind the success of an organization, but it's often a big part of it.

AN INDELIBLE LESSON

For my last three years of high school, I attended a boarding naval academy of several hundred cadets. Although a retired Navy captain coordinated the naval science program, and the Department of Defense assigned three active-duty Navy chiefs to teach there, the school was largely run by cadet officers trained and supported by retired Marines. In my senior year, I served as the battalion executive officer, outranked only by the battalion commander.

Military academies are tightly regimented, and it is the duty of cadet officers, especially line commanders, to preserve this regimentation. In the spring of that year, one of my fellow officers, a company commander, became a significant problem. He began to act up in the mess hall and increasingly encouraged the cadets at his table to do the same. The few faculty and staff members still on campus ate dinner in a private room, so we were on our own. As battalion exec, the mess hall was my responsibility, so I visited his table several nights in a row, first asking and then telling him to bring it under control. None of this did any good and the unruliness began to spread.

I sought the advice of the director of Naval Science, who advised me to "write him up . . . put him on report." Cadet officers routinely put nonofficers on report, which meant that these unlucky souls had to march off their newly acquired demerits carrying a rifle, half an hour for each one. But, it was exceedingly rare for an officer to write up another officer. His advice worried me because doing so could potentially lead to the company commander forfeiting his commission, which is a big deal in any military organization. The captain assured me that he would not allow this to happen. Because I took it for granted that he would follow through on his promise, I did what he recommended. I'm sure he made this promise sincerely, but I realize in hindsight that he simply didn't have the institutional clout to make good on it.

You can imagine the horror I felt when, at noon formation a few days later, the director of activities showed up and handed the battalion commander what was known as a "special order." These were rare. Only seven or eight were issued in any given year, usually because some homesick cadet had gone AWOL and was therefore dismissed from the academy. Snare drums began to roll, the company commander was ordered front-and-center, and the battalion adjutant read the order, which stripped the troublesome officer of his commission. In that world, this was like sending a member of the president's cabinet to federal prison. Worse, he was popular with several cadets who made no secret of the fact that they, too, were counting the days until graduation.

Shortly before evening formation a week later, I returned to my room to find red ink splattered all over my white uniforms. This sort of thing is unheard of in a military school, and I fumed about it through evening mess. Before I dismissed the battalion from the mess hall, I entered the small alcove from which I made announcements, and switched on the microphone. Although I don't remember exactly what I said, my father had died a month before, and I was not at my best.

What I do remember is what the senior English teacher said when we got back to the dorms. He'd heard my threats from the faculty dining room, which had its own speaker.

Jack Noble was a fascinating fellow. He'd graduated from Columbia, worked for a while as a writer for Warner Brothers where he'd met William Faulkner, and was acquainted with the poet Edna Saint Vincent Millay from his New York family's garden parties. Noble had also served as an officer in both the Army and National Guard, so he knew something about leadership.

"That," he said, once we were inside his quarters, "was outrageous! You, of all people, ought to know better." Perhaps because he'd always liked and looked out for me, he was especially upset. "How do you expect them to *trust* you?"

"Trust me? I'm the most trusted officer in the battalion."

Jack Noble stared at me, and for a few long seconds remained silent. Then he said, "They trust you with their wallets . . . but not with their welfare." He meant, I think, that I knew how to get cadets to follow military rules and regulations, but I did not instill within them a sense of personal safety.

There was nothing I could say. He was right. All I knew about leadership was that it involved power. I'd understood almost nothing about winning hearts and minds.

That conversation changed my life. Today, if you were to ask my corporate clients, they would tell you that I am highly trusted, and they would not be talking only about honesty. I now understand a good deal more about leadership than I did in military school, and how much it hinges on trust. Such trust has to do with looking after the interests of others, never leaving them in the lurch, being there when they need you, and often handling problems on their behalf before they even know these problems exist. I'm proud to report that one senior vice president recently told me, more or less out of the blue, that I was the most trusted person she knew.

TASK AND RELATIONSHIP

Executives and managers who have attended business school will tell you that the two fundamental dimensions of management are *task* and *relationship.* They will also tell you that a leader can be high on both, low on both, or high on one but low on the other. The manager who gets along well with everyone but accomplishes little is, of course, the opposite of the one who achieves a great deal but alienates everyone in the process.

Some leaders are what Blake and Mouton describe in their 1964 *Managerial Grid* as "9–9." A 9–9 leader is someone who, on a scale from 1 (low) to 9 (high), is high on both task and relationship. Many are 9–9 when they are not trying to meet a fast-approaching deadline or otherwise under pressure, but when the game heats up their behavior changes, perhaps to 9–5 (high on task, medium on relationship) or even 9–1 (high on task, low on relationship). Others never move beyond a 1 or a 5 on task. At the extreme, there is the 1–1 manager, a pattern that defines the barely employable or outright unemployable. The trust quotients (TQs) of leaders who repeatedly demonstrate either an inability to get things done or a willingness to throw other people under the bus tend naturally to decline, and once eroded these can be difficult to rebuild.

Peers and subordinates may continue to be polite on the surface to 9–1 managers, but underneath they will remain wary. Senior-level leaders may repeatedly assign such managers to jobs that require determination and persistence, but they may refuse to promote them. Niccolò Machiavelli noted, in 1514 when he wrote *The Prince,* that to rule without capturing the hearts of those ruled is a dangerous undertaking, requiring a perfect surveillance system. Such managers can rarely turn their backs because people reflexively undermine and retaliate against those who threaten, bully, or intimidate them. They look for payback opportunities.

The easiest form of payback is jumping ship for another enterprise. This imposes an enormous cost on any organization because of how expensive and time-consuming it is to find and train replacements. Many people, now in their twenties, thirties, and forties have watched their parents unceremoniously escorted to the door. Often, these parents had contributed decades of hard work to a company, only to find themselves out in the cold because of the latest downsizing, right sizing, or wrong sizing. In the eyes of many of today's workers, their parents' companies broke implied contracts, and they are never going to let that happen to them. This is why so many workers are willing to change jobs for only a small increase in compensation. Loyalty can no longer be assumed.

Not everything I'm going to discuss in this book has directly to do with how you treat people. Trust is also fostered by qualities that are not exclusively or even primarily relational. Still, all of the ways to foster trust we're going to examine have at least something to do with interpersonal behavior. Treating people well and wisely amounts to a tremendous, though largely unrecognized, competitive advantage.

This does not mean slacking off and letting subordinates do whatever they like. Work entails toil, and most of us would not choose to work as hard as we do if we didn't have to pay the bills. Part of being an effective leader is finding ways to get others to do things they might not otherwise do, and ideally, to do them enthusiastically. Sometimes what they have to do is difficult, unpleasant, or painful, such as working long hours until a project is completed, but it has to be done.

If an athletic coach allows a team to slide, its members may enjoy the chance to coast for a while, but they are unlikely to have a winning season, and in the end they may come to despise the coach. If, on the contrary, the coach demands everything from a team that it can deliver, its members will respect themselves and their coach, regardless of how often they've lost. They will know they've done their best. People will accomplish far more than you ever thought possible if you make clear that you expect them to. But you have to do it in a way they find inspiring and supportive. They have to believe in you.

IS THERE A SINGLE BEST LEADERSHIP STYLE?

It has long been apparent that no single style is ideal under all circumstances, or in relation to all subordinates. You have to lead one way in the heat of battle—when minutes can make the difference between victory and defeat, and there's little or no time to hold a committee meeting—and another way in peacetime. Similarly, you have to manage immature subordinates differently than you do seasoned ones who are self-sufficient, and to whom you can confidently delegate.

As William J. Reddin[1] and Hersey and Blanchard[2] pointed out, beyond task and relationship there is a third dimension to leadership: situational fit. If a given leadership style is appropriate to the circumstance at hand, it is effective, whereas if it is inappropriate, it is ineffective. One way to demonstrate the value of what Hersey and Blanchard term *situational leadership* is to think about how teams make decisions, a subject to which we should devote some attention.

HOW DECISIONS GET MADE

There are at least four ways a team can arrive at a decision, and which one to use depends on the particular problem or challenge. This way of viewing decision making is more streamlined than Vroom and Yetton's well-known model,[3] which is also worth consulting.

Sometimes meetings are ineffective because those leading them remain muddled about how best to approach decision making. If a meeting is called simply to share information, of course, no decision will be required.

The first way is for the leader simply to decide *autocratically,* by fiat. There are circumstances that require immediate action, when there is no time to sit around a conference table and debate. Wartime commanders

often have to make split-second decisions that can have profound consequences. Procurement specialists sometimes have only a few minutes
to say yes or no to high-stakes closeout offers. And, fund managers may
have only moments to choose among several tactical options. There isn't
always time to get everyone on board.

A second way is for the leader to solicit opinions, and based on this input
to make the decision. Note that the leader still decides. Most routine decisions should probably be made this way. As long as the leader doesn't come
across as having already decided, such a *participatory* approach has the advantage of allowing everyone to feel included and thus it facilitates buy-in.

A third way is to keep struggling until *consensus* is reached. Dictionar-
ies can be ambiguous, so I want to make clear that I don't mean general
consensus, the phrase sometimes used to refer to most people agreeing.
Consensus, as I am using the word, refers to unanimity, to everyone agreeing. Reaching such consensus can be laborious and time-consuming, and
therefore inefficient, and you can't always get there. But for certain decisions, it's worth the investment of time and energy because it tends to
maximize commitment.

Finally, one can decide by *voting* between or among the options, which
can have the unfortunate consequence of leaving those who are outvoted
feeling slighted. There are times when putting a decision up for a vote may
be necessary, but it is usually not the best approach.

Of the four styles of decision making—autocratic, participatory, con-
sensual, and pluralistic—you might think of the first as high task/low relationship, the second as high task/high relationship, the third as high
relationship/low task, and the fourth as low task/low relationship.

But there are nuances. Sometimes, the best way to preserve relationships
is by becoming singularly task-focused. If a combat commander does not
do this, there may be no one left with whom to enjoy a relationship. There
are other times when the task *is* the relationship, when the most important
objective for a cold, detached, and distant manager is to strengthen interpersonal bonds. The best way to approach a decision, like much else in
leadership and management, depends on the realities at hand.

LEADERSHIP, MANAGEMENT, AND ADMINISTRATION

It may be helpful to consider how these three terms and the activities
they represent relate to each other. You cannot be an effective manager
if you're disorganized, have trouble keeping track of activities and people, and fail to approach your job methodically and systematically. To
be a good manager requires, as a threshold condition, being a competent

administrator. Nor can you be an effective leader if you can't manage. In addition to administrative ability, management requires the capacity to prioritize, assign the right people to the right jobs, run projects so they come in on time and within budget, and ensure the prudent distribution of resources—to plan and execute so that results are achieved. The ability to manage is, in part, what inspires others to follow.

To put this in technical language, management is *nested within* administration, and leadership is nested within management (see the Venn diagram in Figure 1.1). You can be an excellent administrator without being a good manager, and you can be a superb manager without being a good leader. You might think of good administrators as meticulous, good managers as prudent, and good leaders as inspirational.

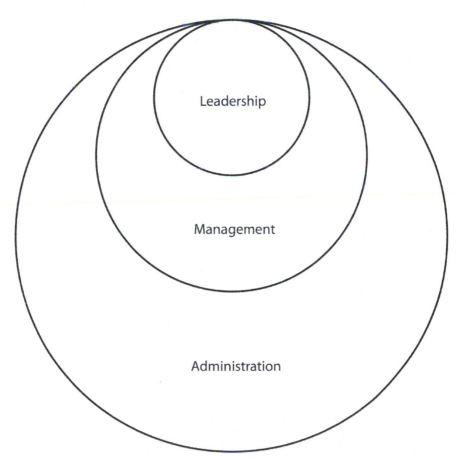

Figure 1.1   Leadership, Management, and Administration

IS TRUST ALWAYS NECESSARY?

If you're selling solar panels door to door, it may not make much difference whether the customer believes you to be fully trustworthy. To buy the panels, he or she has only to be convinced that you will honor whatever agreement the two of you come to, the enterprise you represent is capable of installing the panels, and the benefits to be derived from owning solar panels outweigh their cost. Beyond that, it matters little what the customer thinks about your competence or character, the two domains of trust around which this book is structured. In all long-term relationships within an organization, however, building trust in both domains is indispensible if you want to become a strong leader.

In an insightful talk given to members of the Department of State's Foreign Service on its Economic Bureau's "Leadership Day," March 7, 2012, former Ambassador Charles Ries offered these comments on the central importance of trust by a leader. It also conveys confidence in that leader and is therefore a striking example of how powerful two-way trust can become:

> I picked up special insights working for Admiral Bill Crowe, who was my Ambassador in London in the mid 1990's. Admiral Crowe had been a four-star admiral, combatant commander in the Pacific, and Chairman of the Joint Chiefs of Staff before becoming Ambassador to the Court of St. James . . . Admiral Crowe's basic assumption was that his heads of section knew how to do their jobs. He saw his task as helping . . . while standing by to tackle those challenges where the Embassy especially needed his leadership . . . He was accessible to any of us for guidance and wisdom, but didn't try to tell us how to crack the egg. He trusted we would know, or figure it out . . . Admiral Crowe concentrated on the things he was able to do by empowering his team . . . By trusting them, he cleared his vision to do what only he could do.

We will return to the subject of empowerment in Chapter 15.

MAKING THE CONNECTION

The essence of communication is not speaking with the poise and diction of a Shakespearean actor. Many courses in public speaking mistakenly emphasize something along these lines: enunciate clearly, project your voice, and don't fidget or rock from side to side. As useful as these guidelines may be, I have seen at least one previously natural and gifted communicator ruined by rigidly trying to follow them. Whereas earlier he had been easy and natural, he became stiff and stilted under the tutelage of an actor who fancied himself a speech coach. The essence of communication is not the mechanics of delivery but, rather, *connecting* with your audience. Leadership involves connecting in a way that *facilitates change.* As a result of this kind of connection, the leader inspires others to take action and, often, to do what they might not otherwise choose to do.

How, exactly, does such a connection get established? By building trust along the two axes I will outline in the next chapter. From the vantage point of a subordinate or peer, this is the logical progression:

TRUSTING → CONNECTING → FOLLOWING

A PREVIEW OF WHAT LIES AHEAD

I am going to discuss the implications of two lines of research. Together, they amount to a formidable platform for effective leadership. The first one has been developing for well over half a century, while the second has been around for only a few decades. Each implies five strategies for increasing leadership effectiveness. You can ignore them only at your peril.

Research tradition #1: If you comb through a good dictionary, you will find thousands of words that describe behavior. These words are frequently overlapping and often ambiguous, and they sometimes have several distinct meanings, which leads to this question: Can this verbal chaos be simplified? Are there a small number of basic ways to account for how people act, ways that predict success or failure? The answer is yes and they have come to be known as the *Big Five.* Here they are: intellect, stability, conscientiousness, friendliness, and assertiveness—knowing when to lead and when to follow.

Each of the five has important implications for building trust. And, they are pretty much independent of each other. I'll describe in a later chapter what such independence means and why it is important. The February 2013 catalogue of books published by the American Psychological Association refers to the five-factor model as "the most heavily researched and empirically supported dimensional model of general personality structure."

I once did a large project for a best-in-class American corporation. It was to build an executive selection framework and a set of processes to go along with it. Because I had taught in a PhD program, I knew the research literature well, so I enthusiastically agreed to do the work. Part of it involved interviewing, in depth, either the top human resources executive, or the senior executive to whom this person reported, for over thirty of the nation's most prominent enterprises. Every one was a household name, and most had been celebrated in the popular press as a model in its industry.

In doing the interviews, I was amazed at what seemed to be the haphazard nature of most selection practices. The majority of the companies had arrived at their selection criteria by sitting around a conference table and sharing opinions about what made for success in their organizations, as if no other organization on earth was like theirs. One company listed over ninety attributes it screened for, and there was no accompanying statement identifying which of the ninety was more important and which less. If a decision maker believed that number seventeen was most important, whether or not this was true, and that decision maker was the most powerful or influential person in the room, attribute seventeen was going to count a great deal.

Very few of these enterprises came anywhere close to focusing on the Big Five. They might have stumbled onto one or two, but only a single company (3M) had converged on all of them. I continue to marvel at this accomplishment, since I was told they relied on no professional help.

There is certainly a place for determining what tends to work well in a particular organization, and therefore screening for it in those you hire or promote. In some enterprises, getting along well with others is important, while in others being able to argue a position persuasively is the path to success. Still, a great deal of behavioral science suggests that the attributes represented in the Big Five, taken together, are predictive of long-term success in any organization. I will devote a separate chapter to each of the five.

Research tradition #2: The second line of research began in earnest with Peter Salovey,[4] a psychologist at Yale who built on the work previously carried out by Howard Gardner and others. Salovey, like Gardner, was interested in unconventional kinds of intelligence, in what is sometimes known as emotional intelligence. Such savvy is sometimes more important than conventional intelligence, the sort measured by IQ tests. Daniel Goleman first brought this to the attention of the general public in 1995.[5]

Years ago, I conducted an assessment of a candidate for a significant management position. He had graduated first in his class from a prestigious college. At the beginning of the process, I explained, as I routinely do, that no one ever answers all the questions correctly. Many of these questions come from the gold standard of intelligence measures, which is comprised of up to fifteen subtests; other questions require complex problem solving and are closely timed. No one can finish all of the items. Or, so I believed at the time.

He completed everything and all of his answers were correct. When we'd finished, I jokingly thanked him for validating my scoring keys, to which he replied, "a few of those were tricky." Indeed! Except for a few people who work at the nation's flagship think tank where I consult, he might be the smartest person I've ever met. But, he didn't get the job. The company passed on him because, bright as he was by conventional measures, they concluded that he was less than astute in other ways we'll discuss in Part II. Like the research on the Big Five, the work on interpersonal effectiveness (IE) has suggested five strategies for building trust: insight, restraint, nobility, compassion, and, persuasiveness. I will also devote a chapter to each of these.

KNOWING HOW VERSUS KNOWING THAT

Philosophers talk about the difference between *knowing how* and *knowing that.* You could spend three lifetimes learning about gear ratios, leverage principles, and the gyroscopic effect, but none of this knowledge would get you any closer to being able to ride a bicycle. The same sort of thing could be said for swimming, driving, sailing, horseback riding, and countless other skills. An aptitude is the potential to learn something, and you may have plenty of aptitude, whereas an ability is knowing how to do it. When it comes to building trust and therefore to being an effective leader, don't remain stalled at the level of aptitude. Turn your aptitudes into abilities.

No one can acquire mastery without diligence, which puts me in mind of the violinist, wandering around the streets of New York, who finally asks a stranger, "How do you get to Carnegie Hall? To which the stranger replies, "practice, practice, practice." Some of the strategies I'm going to recommend may already be second nature to you, while others may feel alien. Focus primarily on the latter.

Winners lose more often than losers. If you try to sell 100 refrigerators, but succeed only 10 percent of the time, you will have failed ninety times. If, at the same rate of success, you attempt to sell only ten refrigerators, you will have failed only nine times. But, in the first instance you will have sold ten refrigerators, and in the second only one.

Be a winner.

TWO

Axes of Trust: Competence and Character

Soon after beginning to work as a management consultant, I realized how many managers are more or less oblivious to the importance of building trust. They seem to regard it as either an elective, a nice-to-have, or as irrelevant to getting real work done.

Some rely almost exclusively on position power, on their place in the hierarchy, as if occupying a specific box on the org chart is all they needed. This is rarely the case, and those who major in command-and-control to the exclusion of enfranchisement almost always end up paying for it.

Other managers delude themselves into believing that strategic vision is all that's required, as if everything depended on forward thinking. As important as such thinking is, research has demonstrated that the person with the best ideas is not necessarily the best leader, which is why, over half a century ago, psychologists began to talk about two kinds of leaders, one *task* and the other *social*.

Still other managers focus only on building morale, perhaps handing out coffee mugs, t-shirts, and monogrammed lollipops. They're terrific cheerleaders. But they sometimes completely neglect other qualities important in leaders—such as being creative and, often most important of all, conscientious.

Leadership is, at root, the creation of followers. Great leaders almost always demonstrate the same array of traits. One leader may be stronger on trait X, while another may be stronger on trait Y, but you can be sure both leaders will demonstrate both X and Y. George Washington, Abraham Lincoln, and Winston Churchill had decidedly different personalities. All three were confident, of course, and it is important to keep in mind that if you don't display self-confidence, no one else is likely to have confidence in you either. But, self-confidence is not enough, not in the long run. All three—and every other great leader who's ever lived—showed the characteristics we will discuss.

The words *confidence* and *faith* come from Latin terms that mean to rely on completely, to demonstrate loyalty and allegiance to, to be persuaded by, to obey, and to have full trust in. The word *trust* seems to have come from a Scandinavian term meaning to be confident that another person will help you, act responsibly, prove true, and—perhaps most importantly— honor a covenant.

Covenant is an intriguing concept. Although some people use contract and covenant pretty much interchangeably, it is useful to draw a distinction between the two. A contract, at its simplest, means I promise to do something for you, and you promise to do something for me. Covenant, however, is different. It means I will *be* something to you, and you will *be* something to me. Trust is more akin to building a covenant than drafting a contract.

Contracts are by nature concrete. They govern specific actions, and have nothing whatever to do with attitudes, sentiments, and so forth. Their quality typically hinges on documenting, as completely as possible, what members of the legal profession call a *meeting of the minds*. This, in turn, hinges on the contract containing clear definitions and addressing as many contingencies as possible.

By contrast, parties entering into a covenant do not attempt to anticipate all contingencies. A covenant may imply the obligation to do a great many things for, or in relation to, the other person, but such concrete obligations are secondary. Covenants have even more to do with a *meeting of the hearts*. Your effectiveness as a leader hinges largely on how well you can engage people's hearts so that they desire to align their minds. Often, the central question becomes this: *Do you inspire trust?*

VARIETIES OF TRUST

Trust comes in many forms. One kind of trust is when others believe what you say, when they know you don't twist the truth because it's convenient, that you don't lie. This is often what people mean when they say that Sarah is an honest person, or Tom is a man of his word. In one of the companies I consult for, there is a manager whom others view as less than truthful. He'll say one thing to one colleague, and the opposite to another. And, it seems, half the time he doesn't even remember the last version he dished up. Some of them tried to convince themselves he was simply being misunderstood, that the problem was one of communication. They wanted to believe. But the reality eventually dawned on them. As one person told me, "I don't think he even knows he's lying. It doesn't register on him." Having studied organizational dynamics for decades, I believe it's only a matter of time before his reputation will catch up with him. Even if it doesn't, it's unlikely he'll get promoted.

Another type of trust is when other people have confidence in your financial integrity, when they realize you'll be an honorable custodian or steward of their wallets and the company's assets. When they know you do not steal. Those caught embezzling come to be seen as disloyal to the corporate tribe, perhaps even as traitors. I still recall how surprised I was, over twenty-five years ago, when an executive I knew was arrested for insider trading. He had a high-ranking job in accounting and finance and so had access to company information unavailable to the public. He certainly didn't seem like a felon, which is what he became. What he never again became, however, was a financial executive.

A third mode of trust is when people know you'll look after their interests, that they can count on you to care about their well-being. You're not out to use them, or get as much out of them as you can, without regard to what it does to them or their families.

Not long ago, I received a phone call from a senior executive who had become alarmed by how profoundly underweight one of his employees was. From what he told me, it appeared his concern was well founded. He wanted advice about whether to talk with her, and if so, how best to bring up the sensitive subject of weight. I've known this man for many years, and it didn't surprise me that he was appropriately concerned he might say or do the wrong thing, something that would make her condition worse. It was clear that he cared, and I was almost certain she would perceive his compassion. And she did. But I've also seen executives who were callous users, and sometimes bullies who rolled over others in quest of their next bonus. Like liars, they were usually found out, and when they were, it proved career limiting.

A fourth form of trust is when others are willing to follow you because they are confident you know what you're doing. Bumblers don't make good leaders. Some managers seem to carry invisible signs that read, "Don't Follow Me—I'm Lost." If you don't know where you're going, you're likely to end up someplace else, and so will those who are unfortunate enough to work with or for you. If, however, you communicate that you have well-thought-out objectives that make sense, know what needs to be done to reach them, are realistic about what can be achieved given the resources available, have the ability to prioritize, and know how to coach others so that they can perform at their best and contribute everything they can, you are likely to inspire both your coworkers and subordinates. And, perhaps those above you as well. These are but a few of the things we can mean when we use the word *trust*.

DO THEY TRUST YOUR CHARACTER?

For our purposes, I'd like to break down the overarching question—*Do you inspire trust?*—into two others. The first is, do others respect your character? This question brings to mind a number of others. Do your subordinates, peers, and leaders know they can depend on you? Are you there for them, through thick and thin, or only when there's something in it for you? Do others think of you as a person of integrity? Are you ethical? Are you fair and impartial? Do you avoid playing favorites? And, are you credible? One way to phrase this question about perceived character is, Do you have the *moral authority* to lead?

A military officer long ago introduced me to the concept of moral authority and its relationship to leadership. He had been selected to become a future battalion commander. One day he told me that he could no longer expect to command a battalion. "Why? I asked, to which he answered, "Because I've lost the moral authority to lead." Through no fault of his, he found himself in what the military considered a subtly compromised position that effectively ended his career. He left the military.

Leadership is ultimately about impact, and impact depends on perception. If, for whatever reason, others don't see you as having this moral authority, they will no longer respect you, which in turn suggests they will also be reluctant to follow.

DO THEY TRUST YOUR COMPETENCE?

This is the second question. Like the first, it brings to mind several others. Do your subordinates regard you as capable? Do they support and follow you because they have confidence in your ability? Or, do they align with you primarily because of your position power, your place in the hierarchy? Do you lead from the *authority of competence,* or mostly through the authority of position? Do senior leaders trust your competence? How about your peers?

Competence at anything, especially a job with significant responsibility, is not always something that can be measured by a straightforward test. It sometimes derives from a mysterious combination of such other qualities as raw intelligence, relevant experience, and the capacity to remain focused. Competence at almost any high-level job depends on these three characteristics in varying proportions. But, for certain jobs, a lot more may also be required, such as the ability to remain calm under pressure, to form key relationships, or to make difficult decisions with very little information. It might also hinge on your technical expertise, your fund of specialized knowledge. Consider these three examples:

First, unless you've been trained to fly a commercial airliner, you might not do well if you were suddenly dropped into the cockpit at 30,000 feet. Without assistance from someone who knew how to pilot such a craft, your chances of survival would not be promising. Nor would the prospects of anyone else on board. You might become overwhelmed by all the dials and indicators—*task saturated*—which, in turn, could cause you to make poor decisions. The single most important contributor to competence at piloting a particular jet would be prior experience flying it.

Second, suppose you were a laboratory scientist. Your competence might depend on intelligence, as this is conventionally understood and measured, *and* on how much you knew about your discipline. But, in certain areas of science, such as theoretical physics, it might also depend on your intuition—your ability to develop the right hunches, to draw productively on what chemist-turned-philosopher Michael Polanyi called *tacit knowledge.*

Finally, if you were a surgeon, your competence would depend on your working knowledge of anatomy and physiology. But it might also depend heavily on your ability to remain levelheaded under pressure. Your conscientiousness would also be important: surgeons can't have too many bad days. And, stamina would contribute to competency, since surgeries can become complicated, requiring the surgeon to stand for many hours without a lapse of attention. All of these characteristics contribute to surgical competence.

CAPABILITY AND CREDIBILITY

If you enjoy a position of leadership in an organization, whether for-profit or not-for-profit, it is important that you inspire others to follow you.

For this to happen, as suggested earlier, they have to trust your *character* and your *competence*. Otherwise, because of the consequence control you have over them, they may smile to your face, but never give you their allegiance.

If they trust your character but not your competence, they will respect your integrity but not your talent; they will come to view you as good-natured but ineffective, in the worst case a likeable buffoon. If, on the other hand, they trust your competence but not your character, they may regard you as a gifted scoundrel.

Thinking about the intersection of character and competence reminds me of a discussion I once had with the former president of a think tank. A physicist, he had worked in the White House for the National Security Advisor, Zbigniew Brzezinski, and was an expert on NATO and nuclear deterrence. The think tank president mentioned, in passing, that deterrence depends on *capability* and *credibility*. A potential aggressor has to believe that you have the capacity to retaliate, should this become necessary, and that you have the political will to do so—that such threats as you issue are not idle.

Although capability and credibility are not precisely the same as competence and character, the two sets of concepts are similar. Competence can be thought of as capability or capacity. And what we are calling character, in its turn, amounts to a certain kind of moral credibility. At root, it means that others recognize you mean what you say, say what you mean, and perhaps at the most general level, consistently do the right thing.

Colin Powell summed up the interaction of competence and character this way: "Leadership is solving problems. The day soldiers stop bringing you their problems is the day you have stopped leading them. They have either lost confidence that you can help or concluded you do not care. Either case is a failure of leadership."[1]

LOOKING AHEAD

We're going to take a detailed look at ten kinds of behavior that inspire trust—ten strategies. Some of them are more important for building trust in competence, and others for building trust in character. A few contribute substantially to both. In Part I, we'll consider the Big Five, qualities that are powerful drivers of performance for everyone from the parking attendant to the CEO. They are the wellsprings from which other important traits flow.

These are the *attributes* that everyone in a position of leadership, to greater or lesser extent, demonstrates. If, instead of calling them attributes, you prefer to think of them as qualities or characteristics, that's fine; it doesn't matter what you call them. What does matter is that you understand how, as you progress in your career, the five become increasingly important.

PART I

Foundations for Building Trust

THE BIG FIVE

Intellect: Conceptual thinking; analytic and intuitive reasoning; understanding complex ideas; realistically thinking about strategy and tactics; and seeing the big picture without getting bogged down in trivia.

Stability: Emotional maturity and predictability; acting like an adult as opposed to a child; and not allowing moodiness or temporary emotional states to intrude into your organizational behavior.

Conscientiousness: Taking the initiative; acting responsibly; demonstrating sustained effort; not becoming sidetracked; closing when appropriate; and getting things done.

Friendliness: Acting in a collegial and helpful manner; avoiding opportunistic or predatory behavior; and being able to establish and maintain long-term collaborative relationships.

Assertiveness: Leading when appropriate; following when doing so is more functional; and acting neither rigidly dominant nor chronically unsure, hesitant, or timid.

THREE

Introduction to the Big Five

Many approaches to leadership emphasize a single trait, often to the exclusion of others. Some, for example, stress the importance of intelligence—one of the Big Five. Intelligence is certainly a major part of the story. But it is by no means all of it.

As we will see, other attributes of a person can seriously interfere with the effective use of raw intelligence. An otherwise gifted manager may, for example, demonstrate abysmal judgment and, as a result, cripple or ruin an organization. The question, of course, is why this happens. What's going wrong? This is where the Big Five proves exceedingly helpful.

It is now possible to identify *patterns* of traits that foster effective leadership or its absence. By looking at two or more of the Big Five together, it is often possible to understand precisely why a particular leader succeeds or fails. Single-trait theories preclude such understanding. Their advocates fail to grasp the extent to which a small *collection* of interacting traits accounts for a great deal of what people do.[1]

I want to emphasize that these five traits were discovered, not invented. No armchair theorist pulled them out of the air, and no group of managers dreamt them up sitting around a conference table. For over seventy years, empirical research has demonstrated the robustness of the five-factor model.

DEVELOPMENT OF THE BIG FIVE

As noted in Chapter 1, any good English dictionary contains thousands of words that describe how people act. Most of them have multiple meanings, are therefore ambiguous, and frequently overlap. But, until the necessary research was done, it was not clear how. Does *active,* for example, mean currently in motion, disinclined to be passive, or generally energetic? What about *social?* Does this mean eager to accept invitations to parties, or merely outgoing?

We know that between 5,000 and 7,000 such terms exist because in the 1940s a Harvard psychologist named Gordon Allport had them counted. This led to the question of whether, using the right analytic methods, all these terms could be boiled down to a few basic ones. If so, how many would there be, and what should they be called? Finally, how accurately would these wellsprings—*source traits*—predict human behavior, including personal and professional effectiveness? How might these traits, taken together, account for success or failure? A source trait, as I am defining it, is one that accounts in an important way for how people act. You might think of it as a root cause.

The answer to the first question—how many—turned out to be five.[2] This was good news. Consider how unwieldy it would have been if the answer ended up being fifteen or twenty. The second question, having to do with how to label the five, is still a matter of controversy, but not nearly enough to prevent us from using the power of the five-factor model. As to the third question—how well the model accounts for what people actually do—the five, when used together, cover a surprisingly large part of the behavioral waterfront. Given the complexity of human behavior, it is unlikely that we will ever be able to predict it anywhere near perfectly, and I would argue that, in principle, perfect prediction is impossible. Still, when you take all five factors into account, it becomes easier to understand why Ted is well liked but can't seem to get things done, while Alex reaches his goals but is without friends or allies. Or, why Ashley rarely talks in meetings, while Teresa routinely speaks up.

When the original research on wellsprings was conducted, each one had to pass a stringent test: it was not allowed to overlap with the others. Or, if it did, such overlap had to be so minor that, for all practical purposes, the overlap could be ignored. They had to be *independent* of one another.

THE POWER OF THE BIG FIVE

Independence is shorthand for *mathematical independence.* This implies that if I know how high or low you are on any one of the five, it tells me little or nothing about how high or low you are on the other four. The Big Five are so fundamental and their overlap so trivial that we can assume them to be *uncorrelated:* we cannot predict where someone is on any one of them simply by knowing where he or she is on the others, either alone or in combination.

Suppose, for example, I know you to be highly intelligent. You approach problems logically and are good at abstract thinking and analytic problem solving. Based on knowing this alone, would I be able to determine in advance how stable you are (Chapter 5), how reliable (Chapter 6), how friendly (Chapter 7), or how assertive (Chapter 8)? You might turn out to be stable or unstable, responsible or irresponsible, friendly or unfriendly, and assertive or unassertive.

To borrow an expression from the oil industry having to do with drilling platforms, many of us know highly intelligent people who are not completely bolted down. They are moody, irritable, erratic, unpredictable, and either riddled with anxiety or incapacitated by depression. We also know gifted people who are admirably mature and well balanced.

Turning to the issue of motivation, some very smart people are irresponsible, lazy, unfocused, and unmotivated. They may flunk out of school to everyone's amazement, perhaps even their own. But other smart people are diligent, conscientious, and goal-directed. To their raw intelligence, they add the turbo-booster of unwavering commitment.

What about friendliness—collegiality? Some gifted people establish and maintain lifelong friendships, while others either can't seem to make friends, or if they do, can't seem to keep them.

Finally, think about assertiveness and how it relates to intelligence. You can be intelligent and rigidly assertive, chronically unassertive, or assertively flexible, sometimes leading and other times following. It's impossible to predict assertiveness from how smart you are. It is this mathematical independence that makes the Big Five so powerful.

The truly impressive thing is if you know where an individual is on all five, you will be able to account for a great deal of what that person does. When viewed as a pattern or profile, the Big Five can substantially help make sense of a lot of the differences you observe in people. The five-factor model is simple to use, yet it yields impressive—and surprisingly powerful—results.

If we use only three levels—low, medium, and high—to rate people on each of the Big Five, it is possible to come up with 243 profiles. To compute how many profiles are possible, simply multiply $3 \times 3 \times 3 \times 3 \times 3$.[3] Suppose, however, that we use five levels for our ratings, perhaps high, medium high, medium, medium low, and low. This time, to figure out the total number of possible profiles, multiply $5 \times 5 \times 5 \times 5 \times 5$. The total number of possible profiles this time turns out to be a staggering 3,125.

The five-factor model is deceptively simple, since it allows for more variation between and among people than may be immediately apparent. As mentioned in Chapter 1, in the 1990s I developed an executive selection system for a large company. It was based on using five levels for each trait in the Big Five. The company's senior executive in human resources wanted future promotion decisions to be made more objectively, and the first application of the system was to identify who among current managers should become the next vice president. One person immediately rose to the top of the list. She just retired as CEO of that company! It is unlikely she would have even been noticed at that early point in her career, had it not been for the rigorous use of the Big Five.

LIMITS TO MATHEMATICAL INDEPENDENCE

The components of the Big Five are, as stated earlier, pretty much independent of one another, so that any overlap between them is minor. This is certainly true for the vast majority of people who function as leaders in organizations. They do not typically show any obvious psychiatric impairment, their behavior is substantially governed by conventional norms, and their perceptions of the world are more or less normal.

Mathematical independence among the five factors does not always hold, however, for people whose behavior is extreme. Consider the relationship between stability and intelligence. Some people are so troubled that they cannot think clearly. Their minds are flooded with profoundly disturbing or intensely confusing thoughts. They might, for example, hear voices, or find themselves plagued by paranoid preoccupations. Serious mental disorganization is likely to lower functional intelligence.

Major defects in stability may also cause decreases in friendliness. Disturbed and confused individuals almost always have disturbed and confused relationships. Because others cannot be sure what unstable people will do from day to day, or even minute to minute, their friendships are often impaired. There may be painful fights. Or, others may back away because they tire of the unstable person's pervasive negativity, overwhelming anxiety, or deeply depressed moods. This, in turn, is likely to make the unstable person less friendly.

These are but two examples of how, at the extremes, independence between and among the factors breaks down. Most people you come in contact with inside an organization are unlikely to show these sorts of behavioral extremes, however, so for our purposes it makes sense to assume that the components of the Big Five are, in fact, mutually independent and, thus, do not correlate with each other.

OUR APPROACH

For each of the ten strategic paths to building trust discussed in this book, I will first pose a set of general questions for your reflection. Then, in the chapter dedicated to each path, we'll consider why your answers to these questions are important to your effectiveness as a leader.

When we have completed our discussion of the first five (Part I), I'll present some of the more interesting profiles I've identified over the years (Chapter 9). Because these profiles will probably make intuitive sense to you—"Ah, that really captures Bob" or "Now, I understand what's going on with Alice"—they will help demonstrate the extraordinary power of the Big Five, both as a tool for making sense of how others act, as well as for your development as a leader.

FOUR

Intellect: Conceptual Thinking and Intuitive Reasoning

Do you demonstrate strong conceptual thinking, solid analytical reasoning, and sound judgment? What about intuition, and knowing when and when not to rely on it? Can you translate abstract ideas into realistic strategies and tactics? Do you show practical intelligence? Are you open to advice and consultation?

We'll begin this chapter with a light-hearted story, but one with a serious message. A man goes out onto the ice to go fishing. He takes his brace and augur bit, and begins to drill a hole. Suddenly he hears a voice, "Do not cut the ice . . . there are no fish under there." He looks around, doesn't see anyone, and begins to drill again. A second time the voice comes out of nowhere, "I told you, do *not* cut that ice . . . there are *no* fish under there!" Once more, he looks around, but still doesn't see anybody. Who is it? He wonders. His neighbor? Maybe it's his mother-in-law. Not to be dissuaded, he picks up the tool a third time and begins to drill. The voice immediately booms, "I told you, do *not* cut that ice . . . there are *no* fish under there!" Startled, the man looks up. "Is that you, God?" To which the voice responds, "No! It's the rink manager!"

You may know a few otherwise intelligent people who, like the man in our story, persist in doing things that don't make sense. They have high IQs, but their *functional intelligence* is at best modest.

TESTS, GRADES, AND INTELLIGENCE

Our focus in this chapter is not on academic ability. A lot of people earn good grades in school and do well on tests. But, they have little common sense, and they're not especially creative. Nor are they particularly open to new ideas: "My mind's made up, don't confuse me with the facts." They tend to get bogged down and suffer from hardening of the categories. Or, they complexify everything, so that very little is simple or straightforward. Some show an instinct for the capillary—they get lost in details and miss the big picture. Strategic thinking is not their strong suit, and they are not quick to see patterns, implications, or trends. Nor do they engage in much possibility thinking—the kind that wonders what, in the future, might be created out of what now exists. Their capacity to connect the floor of the concrete with the ceiling of the abstract leaves something to be desired, they are not especially insightful, and, as the following example illustrates, they are largely bereft of practicality. Most significantly, they are unlikely to show good judgment, which in the end is what every leader gets paid for. As Peter F. Drucker put it, "Management is doing things right; leadership is doing the right things."

A few years ago, in a company that is well known in its industry, I began to try to help one of its executives. He had credentials that glowed in the dark—elite schools, top of his class, academic honors, scholarships, you name it. In an attempt to provide him with more insight about himself, I collected anonymous written feedback from co-workers on a guest list he and I had developed. This is one of the comments that came in: "He fails to articulate strategies and tactics, I think because he doesn't see the connections." Here's another: "He needs to stop jumping from one idea to the next." One of his subordinates wrote, "We need plans we can execute, not more higher theoretical thinking . . . he gets lost in the cosmos." He was not inspiring much trust in his competence. When he made decisions, his subordinates had little confidence that he had evaluated all reasonable options, carefully weighed the risks and benefits, and come up with a plan that made practical sense.

Incompetently reckless officers in the military occasionally get fragged in combat, which is military jargon for being assassinated by your own men: shot in the back or thrown a live grenade. Their men rarely like them, but more to the point, are strongly reluctant to follow them.

WHAT IT DOES AND DOESN'T MEAN TO BE INTELLIGENT

Researchers who study the Big Five sometimes think of this first dimension as open-mindedness. A few refer to it by the seemingly odd term *culture.* They do not mean by this that a person high on factor one spends Saturdays at the museum and Sundays at the symphony. By high on culture they mean remaining alert and well attuned to what's going on, having what might be called a circumspect view of society and, more broadly, the world. For over a hundred years, industrial psychologists have emphasized that intelligence is a strong predictor of success. The question becomes how, exactly, intelligence should be defined and measured, how narrowly or broadly.

When I began teaching doctoral students, I quickly noticed that some who had done very well on the Graduate Record Examination (GRE) were not especially good at conceptual thinking. To be among the best thinkers, a student typically had to have solid scores on the GRE, but such scores were no guarantee that he or she was a strong conceptualizer. Over the past few decades, psychologists have shed more light on why this is so.

In 2002, Daniel Kahneman of Princeton University won the Nobel Prize in Economics for his analysis of human judgment and decision making. In 2011, he published a book titled *Thinking Fast and Slow* that elegantly demonstrates how even people with high levels of measured intelligence can make egregious errors. He describes a kind of thinking that is fast, instinctive, and emotive, and another that is slower, more deliberative, and more logical. Both work together, for good or ill, to influence our judgments and decisions.

Paying homage to the work of Kahneman and his deceased collaborator Amos Tversky, Keith Stanovich came out in 2009 with *What Intelligence Tests Miss.* In it, he delivered an important message, one that for decades had been emphasized in materials that accompany the Wechsler Adult Intelligence Scale (WAIS). The WAIS is an individually administered IQ test that is preeminent for measuring mental ability. It consists of ten core subtests, plus five supplemental ones, and it takes at least an hour of face-to-face time to administer. The following statements appear in the technical manual that accompanies the latest version of the WAIS:

> Performance on measures of cognitive ability reflects only a portion of what comprises intelligence [which is the] capacity of the individual to act purposefully, to think rationally, and to deal effectively with his environment . . . [intelligence should not be defined] in pure cognitive terms . . . another group of attributes [contribute to intelligent behavior, including] planning and goal awareness, enthusiasm . . . and persistence. Such attributes are not directly tapped by standardized

measures of intellectual ability, yet they influence . . . [the individual's] effectiveness in daily living.[1]

The intellect discussed in this chapter, therefore, is much broader than what the SAT or grades measure. It's, rather, a certain keen-mindedness that people who do well in school or on tests do not always demonstrate.

THE SMARTEST GUY IN THE ROOM CAN'T BE

Effective leaders will often tell you that they try hard to surround them-selves with people who are smarter than they are. Having the sense to do this is far more important than IQ scores. It's a pretty good bet that the leader who recruits and retains the most talent, rather than fretting about being outclassed, is strong on conceptual thinking and analytic reasoning. He or she also probably shows overall good judgment. Effective leaders know when to ask for advice, which is part of what it means to be intel-ligent. This is why some researchers call this first characteristic *openness,* by which they mean openness to the input of others and to novel experi-ences, including new ways of looking at problems.

The smartest person in the room can't be, almost by definition. Peo-ple who waste an inordinate amount of airtime telling everyone else how much they know unwittingly shut themselves off from potentially useful information. It's hard to talk and hear at the same time. Great leaders are almost always good listeners.

ON NOT BECOMING AN *IDIOT SAVANT*

An *idiot savant* is a term, no longer used by psychologists, to refer to someone whose intellectual capacities are severely limited except in one distinct area. Such a person may not know how to spell simple words or use a telephone but can instantly tell you on what day of the week Sep-tember 3, 2063, falls. Or, what the product is when you multiply 4,019 by 61,212.[2] I am using this label as a metaphor for a certain kind of dysfunc-tional leader.

A high-ranking executive who once worked for one of the companies for which I've consulted was universally viewed as highly intelligent. By ordinary measures, no doubt he was. But his level of operational intel-ligence was less than ideal. He would dive down into matters that should have been handled by managers far below him in the organization, if for no other reason than that they were more knowledgeable about them. His deep diving would periodically cause commotion within the company. It also contributed to a lot of inefficiency, and upset those with more subject-matter expertise who, perhaps out of fear, were reluctant to say so. Worst of all, wasting his time in this fashion prevented him from adding value where he legitimately might have. Each of us has only so much free mental space, and when it's wasted on relatively trivial matters, there may be little left over for what's truly important. It was more than obvious that he was not a good time manager, which implies that he was not a good *task* manager. But, he had a more serious deficiency.

To this executive, everything was a spreadsheet. He seemed to believe that all problems and challenges could immediately be reduced to a set of concrete numbers. Clearly, he was skilled at analytic problem solving, an important component of intellect. But it is not the only one. All good leaders show the capacity to reason analytically *and* intuitively, and he was almost entirely devoid of ability to do the latter.

ANALYTIC AND INTUITIVE REASONING

I first realized there were two different modes of thinking when I was consulting for a manufacturing company. But I had never come across a discussion of the two modes and the difference between them, either in a book or in school—until I read Malcolm Gladwell's 2005 book *Blink*. He quotes a United States Marine Corps officer describing how he and his fellow officers analyzed the outcome of a training exercise in an after-action review (AAR); during such AARs, it is common for the unit to attempt to identify three things that went well and three that didn't. Gladwell reports Paul Van Riper to have said, "When we talk about analytic versus intuitive decision making, neither is good or bad. What is bad is if you use either of them in an inappropriate circumstance." Here is how I have come to think about the difference between these complementary but essential modes of thinking:

With analytic reasoning, you know the options, the dimensions or variables on which to evaluate these options, and you pretty much know how much to weight each variable. Suppose, for example, you had to decide which of three job offers to accept, each with a different company. Let's call the companies X (located in New York), Y (located in Los Angeles), and Z (located in Atlanta). How might you go about making the decision analytically?

You could make a list of what's important to you in a job, such as the size of the company, the industry it's in, where the job is located, level of the job, compensation and benefits, amount of travel required, prestige of the enterprise, and educational institutions in the vicinity. Then, you might decide how much emphasis to put on each of them—how much weight to give each dimension of evaluation (characteristic or quality), say on a scale from 1 (low) to 5 (high). It might be twice as important for you to work at a company near a college or university so you could take classes at night than to work for a prestigious firm. And, it might not matter much where the company was located. So, you might assign a weight of 4 to *access to educational institutions* (educational access), a weight of 2 to *prestige of the enterprise* (prestige), and a weight of 1 to *where the job is located* (location). You would, of course, also assign a weight to each of the other dimensions you'd listed.

Then, you could rate each job on each dimension, say from 1 (low) to 5 (high). To keep our example simple, we'll continue to use only the three dimensions just cited. Let's say that you rated the job with Company X this way: 5 on *access to educational institutions* (since it is located close to a university), 3 on *prestige of the enterprise,* and 4 on *where the job is located.* We'll further assume that the corresponding ratings you gave to the job at Company Y were 5, 4, and 1, and for the one at Company Z, 4, 4, and 3.

If you then multiplied each rating by the *weight* (W) you'd already assigned that dimension, you would get a *product* (P) for each job on each of the three dimensions. For Company X, you'd end up with 5 (rating) × 4 (weight) = 20, 3 × 2 = 6, and 4 × 1 = 4, for a total of 30. Doing the same for Companies Y and Z would give you corresponding totals of 29 for Y and 27 for Z. Note that the weight for each dimension remains constant—for all three job offers, it is always 4 for *access to educational institutions,* 2 for *prestige of the enterprise,* and 1 for *where the job is located* (see Table 4.1).

Table 4.1   Using Analytic Reasoning to Choose Among Job Opportunities

Job	Educational Access (Rating)	W	P	Prestige (Rating)	W	P	Location (Rating)	W	P	Total
X	5	4	20	3	2	6	4	1	4	**30**
Y	5	4	20	4	2	8	1	1	1	**29**
Z	4	4	16	4	2	8	3	1	3	**27**

This table is only partially complete because we originally listed eight dimensions for evaluation, and we've computed and displayed the results for only three. The column to the far right, therefore, actually contains only subtotals. You'd have to carry out these sorts of ratings and calculations for the three companies on the other five dimensions you'd initially determined to be important. This would allow you to come up with a grand total for each of the three offers. The one with the highest grand total would be the one you'd determined, analytically, to be most attractive.

Naturally, you'd have to review this entire procedure, to make sure you hadn't neglected something important, but in general this is how analytic reasoning works. The process is by nature explicit. Some subjectivity is involved in coming up with what's important to you in a job, in assigning a weight to each of the dimensions, and in rating each of the jobs on these dimensions. But, the procedure is primarily a conscious one. Little or nothing is going on unconsciously.

Intuitive reasoning is different. It's what we usually mean when we say, "my gut tells me" or "instinctively I know this is right." In making a decision intuitively, you might well take into account scores of variables you're unaware of. You can't name these variables if you don't know what they are, and if you can't name them, how could you possibly assign weights to them? The majority of innovations, either in science or business, probably come about through intuitive leaps, which reflects how intuitive decision making is partly an unconscious process. Below are two examples of elegant intuitive reasoning, one from business and the other from science.

Whatever else people might have thought or said about Jack Welch, he was brilliant as a CEO when he decided that General Electric would be either number one or two in a particular business or get out of it. This strategy worked well to increase what fell to the bottom line for GE.

But who told Jack Welch that? Did tablets fall from the sky? Why not stay in any business if you're number one, two, or three? Or, perhaps stay in a business only if you dominate the market, if you're number one? Some approaches to strategic decision making might have led to a course of action different from the one that seemed intuitively correct to Jack Welch. Because the decision was largely intuitive rather than analytic, I suspect that even he would not be able to explain fully how he reached it.

Here's the example from science: In the early 1900s, an unknown scientist was working in a patent office because he couldn't get a university job. He'd been thinking for years about gravity, time, and space, and the relationship between them. He mused, for example, about why the light emanating from the headlamp of a train, speeding along at eighty miles an hour, didn't go 80 mph *plus* 186,000 miles a second—but, still, only 186,000 miles per second. And, about riding up and down in elevators, and whether, as you went faster in space, you would age more quickly or slowly. In 1905, Albert Einstein, that unknown scientist, published three seminal papers that changed the landscape of physics.

I should perhaps add that, according to Michael Polanyi in his 1958 book *Personal Knowledge,* it is a myth that Einstein came to his theory of relativity from noticing persistent inconsistencies in the experiments of Michelson and Morley to measure the speed of light, a myth still commonly taught in textbooks. In reality, he'd been intuitively pondering the nature of space and time since he'd been a teenager.

ANALYSIS AS A CHECK ON INTUITION

On one hand, analysis is unlikely to replace intuition as a source of creative ideas and therefore as the wellspring of innovation. On the other, if any of us had infallible intuition, which none of us do, we would always make the right decision. Analytic thinking would be unnecessary.

Analysis helps run disciplined and systematic checks on intuition, on the wisdom or folly of going down one path as opposed to another. Since none of us has perfect intuition, we need good analysis, the kind you learn to do in business or accounting school. Effective leaders sense what they don't know, and when they need to ask for a sanity check on their hunches.

I once cancelled my subscription to a service because its senior executives had decided to charge separately for services that had previously been bundled together. If I still wanted both services, I'd have to pay substantially more. Wall Street was not kind to them for this new pricing structure, which seems to have been rooted in flawed intuition about how consumers would respond to the change.

Had they done any well-designed market research? Were there any competently run focus groups? Not likely. Market research and focus groups are but two of the ways they might have collected data that, properly analyzed, would have yielded accurate predictive *information.* This, in turn, could have saved their enterprise from a massive, albeit temporary, devaluation.

COMPONENTS OF INTELLIGENCE

1. The first component of intelligent behavior, the kind that inspires trust, is the capacity *to think conceptually.* This, of course, implies the

ability to think logically. Often, you can demonstrate such behavior by proxy, which is to say that, if conceptual thinking is not your strong suit, you can gather people around you who do this well. Or, at least you can ask others for their advice and counsel. If they are your subordinates, their job is to help you do your best, so there's no dishonor in asking for their help, provided you give them appropriate credit. Those above you do not expect you to generate the answers all by yourself, only to come up with them.

Conceptual thinking requires, above all, the ability to define the terms of a discussion in order to avoid ambiguity and detect inconsistencies. To achieve clarity by disambiguation, all you have to do is ask questions, like the television detective Columbo, who routinely introduced his telling question with "just one more thing." A helpful question you can use to achieve additional clarity is, "How do you mean? As any competent psychotherapist will tell you, this works far better than "What do you mean?" since asking "what" often results in mere repetition.

To detect inconsistencies in what others say, listen for contradictions. Nothing can be A and not-A at the same time. Just as individuals sometimes pursue mutually exclusive goals, organizations sometimes do also. I have watched the leader of one enterprise torment himself because it was not growing, only to discover that he seemed unwilling to take on the additional work that such growth would entail.

2. *Skill at information processing and analytical problem solving* is the second component. In Chapter 1, I mentioned the capacity of one CEO in the food manufacturing industry to comprehend and make sense of large quantities of information. He could keep in mind how much of each product his company produced every month and the distribution channels through which it was being delivered. And, he was on top of marketing trends and which of the company's new products were most likely to succeed. This man was gifted at understanding huge data sets and the interrelationships between and among them—if sales of one product rose, to what extent could he expect sales of another to decline? Was such a trade-off desirable, such that the advertising budget for the first product should be increased? Or, would it be better to deemphasize the first to preserve sales in the second? Should the *slotting fees* paid to supermarkets for shelf space and optimal aisle placement be increased? What about free-standing inserts (FSIs) delivered with Sunday newspapers?

If, taking a good look at yourself, you conclude that you are not gifted at information processing and analytic problem solving, or if you have never been taught to do certain kinds of analysis, do not stick your head in the sand. You don't have to be good at everything. All you have to do is make sure the work gets done and pay proper attention to it. It's a good idea to learn something about the sorts of biases that might lead you to ignore unwelcome results. One example of such a perceptual prejudice is what has been called the *confirmation bias*—selectively looking for what confirms your preconceived opinions while ignoring what challenges them.[3]

3. Next, we come to *sound judgment,* which often requires paying due attention to your instincts as well as to all available analyses. Decisions are nearly always made with incomplete and therefore imperfect information, which means you have to do your best to make the most of the information you have. The important thing is not to drift into a world of your own by cutting yourself off from reality, by becoming functionally autistic. Autism, in the most general sense, is living in fantasy instead of reality.

I recall one executive with an elite business school degree who locked himself in his office for ten hours a day and spent nearly all of his time reading trade journals. As useful as it is to know what's going on in your industry, effective leaders pay attention to a lot more than competitive analysis. The executive I have in mind effectively separated himself from his company as it existed, and began to live in a world of his own. This world was largely a figment of his imagination, one he persuaded himself was real, but which was largely a product of fantasy. As a result, executives senior to him ended his relationship with the enterprise—he "left to pursue other interests," which is often code for having been fired.

4. Closely related to sound judgment and often in support of it is the fourth component, *intuition,* which is the ability to sense the lay of the land without benefit of a roadmap. Although intuitive reasoning usually contributes to what any good leader does, I want to mention two areas where it is especially important.

We have already discussed the first one, instinctive decision making—going with what your gut tells you, provided that no available analysis suggests otherwise. Countless careers have been made or destroyed by such decision making, but there is no sure way to avoid it. Sometimes you just have to play a hunch, a phrase that suggests the underlying nature of intuitive decision making: risk-taking. Informed risk-taking perhaps, but the willingness to accept risk nevertheless. Since we usually have to make decisions with flawed information, it's wise to acknowledge this reality, forgive yourself when you make a decision that does not work out, and reckon squarely with the fact that there is a certain amount of what appears to be randomness at work in everyone's life. How much randomness differs from person to person, but it is always there. You can decrease the risk of making bad intuitive decisions by seeking out and factoring in the opinions of those whose judgment you trust. But you will never entirely eliminate this risk.

The other domain in which intuition plays a central role has to do with other people, with relationships. It's the political realm. You have to have the intuitive intelligence to sense what is, and is not, important to another person at any given time, especially those who have *consequence control* over you. We will return to this topic in a later chapter, but I want to point out here that the *bottom line is rarely the bottom line*. No organization is run by robots programmed to function like "rational economic man," a mythological being that even many economists have long since abandoned.

5. Finally, we come to what is sometimes the most important component of intelligent behavior, *knowing when to rely on analysis and when to rely on intuition*. Both are necessary. The question becomes how much weight to give to data that has been transformed into information, and how much to your instincts. It's as if we were at a casino table and forced to place a bet.

STRATEGIC DRIFT

There are many ways to become disconnected from reality and, thus, to accelerate strategic drift: losing sight of your objective and straying off course. As intimated earlier, strategic drift is often the product of self-imposed isolation. One way is to foster this isolation is to discourage others from sharing contrary points of view.

Someone once told me the following story about Saddam Hussein, reported by someone with first-hand knowledge. Saddam once assembled his ministers and generals in a large room, and encouraged them to share their opinions about how the war with Iran was progressing. He suggested that, in the interest of candor, they leave rank at the door. Everyone in the room quickly assured Saddam that the war was going well—everyone except one participant, who offered the contrary opinion that Iraq was not prosecuting the war well at all. Using a .45 caliber automatic, Saddam ended the man's career on the spot—and became still more disconnected from reality.

An even more basic way to remain out of touch in your decision making is not to ask for the views of others in the first place. Many leaders, as they move north in the food chain, become increasingly convinced of the infallibility of their opinions and biases, on everything from organizational strategy to personnel selection. Sound biases, ones that are based squarely on data, are not only useful but necessary. If you did not have a bias for stopping at red lights, you would soon end up in the hospital, or worse. Biases become dangerous and often destructive, however, when they are not data-based, when they are arbitrary and therefore nonrational or even irrational.

Some leaders begin to believe their press clippings, or, more dangerously, the flattery of self-promoting subordinates. In some instances, they merely conclude that their position alone automatically certifies the rightness of their opinions—why else would they have been put into it? This seems to have been the case with the CEO mentioned previously, the one responsible for the decision that resulted in the devaluation of his company. The old idea of the divine right of kings! Such faith in one's infallibility may no longer cost leaders their heads, but it can certainly cost them and their enterprises a great deal.

Finally, you can speed up the drift into ignorance by discounting whatever advice you get through devaluing the source. You can tell yourself that Jeff never knows what he's talking about and Cynthia always does the wrong kind of analysis. These two words, *never* and *always,* are dangerous, since they nearly always never apply. Use them sparingly.

CAN YOU LEARN TO BE SMARTER?

It is commonly assumed that a person cannot change his or her level of intelligence, which psychologists classify as either *fluid* or *crystallized.* Fluid intelligence is the ability to solve novel problems, often of a nonverbal nature, while crystallized intelligence is the ability to draw on previously acquired knowledge or skill to solve problems or answer questions of a verbal or factual nature.

Some of the subtests of fluid intelligence on the WAIS require solving nonverbal puzzles. The ability to come up with these solutions is largely a function of innate endowment. One such subtest requires the person to use red and white blocks to construct designs that match printed models. Another presents pictures of scales with missing weights on one side, and asks the person to choose which weights to place on the other side to balance the scales. Still another requires the examinee to identify which important part is missing from a series of incomplete pictures. These and other subtests measure *perceptual reasoning,* which is central to fluid intelligence. As suggested earlier, this is unlikely to improve dramatically as a result of experience. Yet, if a person has spent a lot of time doing puzzles, performance on these subtests is likely to be better than it otherwise would have been. Even in the domain of fluid intelligence, the right kind of practice can help.

Turning to crystallized intelligence, one of the WAIS subtests asks the person to define a series of increasingly difficult words, such as *egregious.* Another asks for answers to questions that measure general knowledge, such as the temperature at which water freezes or the number of fluid ounces in a quart. A third subtest draws on both fluid and crystallized intelligence. It requires the person to answer questions of general under-standing, such as why voting is important in a democracy or what a prov-erb such as "Not every cloud brings rain" means.

There is no doubt that education, whether formal or informal, enables people to do better on tests of intelligence. This means they also end up with higher IQ scores. Although those who construct and validate tests like the WAIS try their best to make the items *culture fair,* they make no attempt—nor should they—to make them *experience fair.* If educa-tion didn't help people think better, it would make little sense to go to school.

A large number of people who have attended courses to help prepare them for the SAT, GRE, GMAT, MCAT, or LSAT will tell you that, con-trary to claims sometimes made, such prep courses substantially helped them improve their scores. We can, in fact, all become smarter, not just in the sense of acquiring more information, but in the more important sense of improving our conceptual thinking, analytic reasoning, good judgment, and—yes—even our intuition *and* ability to discern how much to rely on intuition and how much on analysis.

Before I was awarded tenure at the graduate institution where I taught, I had to undergo a review of my performance as a professor. This included scrutiny of my effectiveness in the classroom, productivity as a researcher, and overall ability to function as a doctoral-level mentor. I recall one se-nior faculty member remarking that I was the strongest conceptual thinker they had. If this was true, it was only because, for decades, I had trained myself to look for how ideas connected with each other, and even more importantly, to check for inconsistencies between and among them. I was not born a clear thinker. I'd simply taught myself to become one by re-lentlessly checking and cross-checking. You *can* train yourself to become more rigorous and analytical.

As just one example of how this can be done, I learned early on in my training as a psychologist that people often use the same word to mean differ-ent things. So, I got into the habit of asking, over and over, for clarification. Asking such questions will often avoid a great deal of misunderstanding and ensure that everyone involved thinks more crisply and communicates more clearly.

BUILDING TRUST BY ACTING WISELY

As suggested earlier, you do not have to be the smartest person in the room, and it is rarely prudent to look as if you're trying to get other people to see you that way. I know several managers who may never get promoted because at times they leave others feeling stupid. The truth is they *are* generally more insightful than those around them. But they're not building trust.

The smarter you make other people feel, the smarter they will perceive you to be. It is only prudent to make others feel good about themselves by honoring their contributions and, when you can do so sincerely, complimenting them on their insights. To the extent that you treat people appreciatively, they will tend to perceive you as capable. After all, you'd have to be! You recognize their value, don't you?

Regardless of how gracious you are, to get very far in most organizations, sooner or later you have to demonstrate that you have a keen mind. This implies demonstrating good conceptual thinking, analytic reasoning, judgment, and intuition, plus an awareness of when and how much to rely on intuition versus analysis. But again, you don't have to be an expert on everything. Just take whatever steps are necessary to ensure that, however you do it, you get the information you need to arrive at the best decisions. That is what, in the end, it means to be intelligent.

If and when you cannot do this, come clean with those around you and ask for help. The most powerful word in any language is *no,* but the two most powerful words are *help me,* ideally prefaced with *please.* Few people will ignore a straightforward request for assistance, which is what makes the statement "I need your help" so powerful. Those you ask for help will feel honored and respected. Never worry that asking puts you in the one-down position. It may feel as if you're putting yourself down, but in reality you couldn't ask for help unless you were self-confident. Others will respect you and your intelligence infinitely more for doing this than for trying to fake it, which amounts to a kind of lying. Never lie. No one has a good enough memory to be a successful liar.[4]

FIVE

Stability: Mental Organization and Emotional Maturity

Are you emotionally mature? Is your behavior predictable in contrast to chaotic, erratic, or disruptive? Do you see things for what they are, rather than through the lenses of wishes and needs? Are you without major mood swings, incapacitating anxieties, excessive anger, chronic irritability, and disruptive emotional states?

What many people think of as emotional maturity, psychologists tend to view as basic stability. So, I'll use these terms interchangeably.

Some people are erratic and unpredictable. You just never know what they're going to say or do, or what kind of mood they'll be in, if they'll be happy, sad, pleasant, hostile, irritable, angry, or volatile. They can lash out, clam up, fly off the handle, launch into a tirade, and so on, with little or no provocation. And, they rarely worry about whether they upset or embarrass those around them. They may be riddled with anxiety, or so depressed that their gloom, negativity, and pessimism becomes contagious. If urban sprawl can ruin the beauty of a countryside, depressive sprawl can undermine the morale of an organization. Unstable people have a lot of interference going on inside their heads—the signal-to-noise ratio is unfavorable.

As we've noted, the two attributes that most influence performance are ability and motivation, which is why the formula $P = A \times M$ (performance = ability × motivation) is so powerful. This, however, is not the whole story. Some attributes that also powerfully influence performance cannot be subsumed under A or M. These attributes have nothing to do with talent or drive. They function as moderator or *suppressor variables*. I call them this because they can suppress performance, making it difficult for a person to live up to his or her potential.

WHY LEADERS FAIL

Before we begin to discuss how and why suppressor variables can be corrosive, let's briefly consider failures of ability, discussed in the previous chapter, and of motivation, which we'll address in the following one. Some leaders fail because they lack the intellectual capacity to do well. They just cannot get up to speed. An ill-advised superior may have promoted them because they were personable, winsome, socially attractive, or delivered a presentation well. People tend to overestimate the intelligence of good-looking people, so physical appearance may have led to a flawed selection. Perhaps the one promoted was a friend or relation of someone in high places; many companies, some of them household names, have been brought to the brink of ruin by nepotism, and others have been pushed over it. Or, the bench strength in a particular department may have been thin and there was no time to launch an outside search, so out of desperation an unqualified person was advanced. Regardless of what led to the promotion, the one selected didn't have the talent to succeed.

Turning to motivation, other leaders fail because they simply do not work hard enough, and their laziness catches up with them. They fall asleep at the switch. An important contract may have expired without the option to renew having been exercised. Or, they may have repeatedly delivered shoddy work to upper management. Running a business requires the discipline to stick with repetitive activities that, interesting or not, simply have to be done. Success requires determination. Few leaders enjoy reading lengthy reports or preparing tedious budgets, but such activities are often necessary.

When leaders fail, however, it is often for reasons other than lack of ability or motivation. If most of them hadn't already demonstrated acceptable levels of talent and drive, they wouldn't have been promoted to where they are in the first place. What causes the derailment of senior leaders is almost always a deficiency of another kind.

Among the most troublesome suppressors of performance is instability. I recall one senior manager who dug himself deeper and deeper into a hole. He was suspicious, negative, critical, guarded, and obstructive, and he would unnecessarily complicate issues, which resulted in a lot of wasted time, not only for him but also for others. Several of his colleagues reported that they never knew what he was going to do next, and a few said that in their opinion he suffered from some kind of "mental problem." When those above him finally ran out of patience, he too left to pursue other interests. Those with leadership responsibilities are generally stable, but there are exceptions. Over the years, I've watched the careers of a number of intelligent and motivated leaders crash and burn because of instability.

THE VALUE OF EMOTIONAL MATURITY

If others describe you as mature, they probably mean you function on an even keel. You do not let yourself get carried away by emotion; you avoid making irrational decisions and are reflective as opposed to reactive. Thus, you are not quick to take offense, are more or less predictable, and—very important—you remain calm under pressure. They know they can rely on you, which implies they trust you to act rationally.

Some calm people are not so much stable as adrenaline deficient; they couldn't or wouldn't express an emotion if they won the lottery. They are emotionally flat. Still, an important concomitant of stability is the capacity to keep your cool, to manage stress without falling to pieces. Here are the opening words from a well-known poem about maturity by Rudyard Kipling: "If you can keep your head when all about you are losing theirs."[1] Few of us can always do this, of course, but it is important for a leader to demonstrate poise, especially when the going gets tough.

I remember one manager in accounting who was never promoted because she routinely, almost obsessively, fretted about nearly everything. She had a lot going for her—smart, goal-oriented, collegial, and so forth—but she worried and worried, and worried some more. Eventually, she drove her boss to despair, to the point that he would close his door if he thought she was on her way to see him. On those increasingly rare occasions when they did meet, she would pull on him for reassurance, become distressed if she didn't get it, and spend much of the time agonizing over what she should or could have done.

She had been promoted to where she was based on technical competence, but in this job she stalled and perhaps became an example of the Peter Principle: "Employees tend to rise to their level of incompetence."[2] In other words, they get promoted until, unable to perform well, their career progression stalls. You might not immediately think of this woman as immature or unstable, but when a person has the impact on others she did, it's difficult to dismiss this hypothesis.

DISTURBANCE AND DISTURBING OTHERS

A colleague and I once wrote an article in which we ask the reader to imagine that we are sitting by a fireplace on a cold winter evening, discussing the troubling behavior of Smythe, an executive in charge of operations.[3] Because of the swirl generated by Smythe, morale and productivity had sharply fallen off. Finally, we announce almost in unison, "Smythe is disturbed!" We ask the reader to think about what this statement actually means. What, in other words, has led us to say this?

Smythe has come to our attention because his behavior has *disturbed someone else.* Indeed, it seems to have disturbed the whole company. To call Smythe "disturbed" is perhaps no more accurate than to call his co-workers disturbed—they are disturbed by Smythe. The conclusion that Smythe is disturbed, disordered, or what have you, is based on his adverse social impact. No matter how crazy he is, Smythe would not be in trouble if he had managed to avoid upsetting other people. You can believe you're Napoleon or the Virgin Mary as long as you don't tell anyone. It's when you start saying or doing weird things that the turmoil begins.

Disruptive behavior can be profoundly troublesome in any organization. Such conduct tends to bring about bad outcomes for the individual causing the disturbance, as well as for the organization. Although I usually use the metaphor of a tribe or an organism when discussing organizations, it sometimes makes sense to think of them as machines. Machines are complex entities with many interacting parts, and the parts have to work together smoothly for the organization to function. The enemy of any machine is friction. Friction generates heat, and heat causes wear and tear. If the heat becomes intense and prolonged enough, the machine breaks down.

It is difficult to hit on all cylinders when you work for an organization, especially a large one—you will not always be allowed to operate with maximum creativity, and it is essential to make your peace with this. Too much creativity can prove destabilizing. Without creativity, the enterprise would eventually die, but with too much of it, especially if poorly channeled, creativity would cause it to implode, to devolve into chaos. All organizations have to balance the need for new ideas with the capacity to tolerate change.

FAILURE THROUGH DISRUPTION

I once watched a young executive wreak havoc in an organization because his behavior was arbitrary, disturbing, and disruptive. He was initially hired as the vice president in charge of finance for a parent company.

Because the CEO was impressed with him, he was promoted to senior vice president of operations in one of its subsidiaries. At the time, the subsidiary had only two senior vice presidents and no executive vice president, so he had considerable power. As soon as he moved into his new office, he began to visit factories throughout the South. Again and again, someone at one of these factories, often a disgruntled employee, would complain about a policy or procedure, and the executive would issue a decree on the spot that changed it. Sometimes, what he changed had been in place for decades, and almost always there was a good underlying reason for it. But he never took the time or trouble to find out what that reason was. Disorganization ensued. He, too, left to pursue other interests.

The term *creative disruption* had not yet entered the vocabulary of business, so he could not have used it as an excuse. Creative disruption is similar to a term from economics, *creative destruction,* which is most associated with the Austrian American economist Joseph Schumpeter.

Over the past decade, I have seen a lot of inept change rationalized away with, "Things just needed to be shaken up." Or, "I'm just trying to jar them out of their stodgy mindsets." There is a place for creative disruption, but sometimes what passes for it is, in truth, destructive disruption. The executive I've just described majored in it.

UNSTABLE AT THE TOP

Decades ago, two prominent management consultants wrote a book about instability at the top of organizations.[4] They pointed out how the idiosyncrasies or bizarre conduct of many senior leaders destabilized the organizations they led.

I watched with interest as the CEO of a large holding company took it to the edge of bankruptcy. He'd joined the company as its chief financial officer, lured by the prospect of becoming its next chief executive. But, there was a catch. The company had several medium-sized logistics subsidiaries. Its chairman and CEO wanted to add to its portfolio a larger subsidiary. Kings like to become emperors; monarchs typically rule only one country, whereas emperors rule several.

It was tacitly assumed, I believe, that if the CFO were to ascend, he would have to spearhead a significant acquisition. He ended up acquiring a large but financially troubled company in the defense industry. Many observers could make no sense of this acquisition, for at least two reasons. First, the acquired company, though large, was generally regarded as mediocre. Second, there was little or no synergy, no substantial vertical or horizontal integration between any of the existing logistics businesses and the new acquisition.

This was glossed over by claiming that all of its subsidiaries were in the delivery business, which was like responding to the question of how a weed and a tiger are alike by answering they both exist. If you move far enough up the ladder of abstraction, you can always find some commonality between any two entities, even a spaceship and a squash court. The rationale offered for the potential acquisition was therefore silly, but the acquisition was completed, new executives were recruited, and the man became CEO. Then, the quarterly P&Ls started rolling in, each worse than the last, and earnings per share plummeted. Within a year or two, the new CEO retired and a third CEO was installed. He quickly and wisely sold off the defense company. It wasn't long before the holding company was once again restored to financial health.

What happened to turn an otherwise gifted leader into someone whose judgment so badly faltered? Perhaps it was ambition, since he was probably not going to get the top job unless he completed an acquisition. But, that does not explain why he made the particular acquisition he did. Executives who worked closely with him said that he had a fatal flaw: he would not listen to contrary opinions or tolerate opposition. At least one high-ranking person in the strategic planning department was let go because he voiced his negative appraisal of the pending acquisition. There must have been a certain brittleness and insecurity that caused the CEO to ignore counterarguments.

In Chapter 4, we discussed how imprudent it is for leaders to cut themselves off from key sources of information, since this functionally lowers their intelligence. Sometimes such lowering is rooted in perceptual distortion, with seeing the world through the lenses of wishes, dreams, and fantasies. This may well have been what prompted the flawed acquisition. If so, this stands as a striking example of how a deficiency in one domain of the Big Five, in this case stability, can suppress the full expression of another domain, in this instance intellect.

VARIATIONS ON A THEME

There are other forms of less than perfect maturity at the top. The Hay Group, which is a global consulting firm, conducted a study of leadership in the world's most admired companies. One finding surprised me, since I'm often looking specifically for a *sense of urgency* when I evaluate executive candidates. Chief executive officers who are high on "pacing"—driving people to get things done quickly—were generally less effective than their peers. At lower levels, pacing can be an important part of effectiveness, but this is not always the case for CEOs. Sometimes, of course, it is.

"When the Chairman spits, the basement floods" is a witticism aptly applied to CEOs. Another is, "When the CEO sneezes, there's a hurricane in the cellar." Chief executives often lose sight of how much impact they have. What to them is a level 3 on a scale of impact from 1 to 10, may to their subordinates be an 8 or a 9. If they frown at some employees for a reason that has nothing to do with work, perhaps an argument at home, these employees may not sleep that night.

The Hay study concluded that the quality that most distinguished chief executives from their competitors who were passed over was maturity, in particular the self-regulation of expressive behavior, a subject to which we'll return in Chapter 12. Other qualities were also important, such as integrity and empathy, but restraint was by far the most important. An insidious effect of overly expressive CEOs is that they can unwittingly induce paralysis in those below them. This, in turn, can reduce creativity because innovative thinking often requires the mental freedom to become absorbed in a problem. This is hard to do if you're preoccupied with concerns about survival.

MANAGING WORRY

It has been said that if you have a job without problems, you don't have a job. We all worry. And, leaders use different ways to bind their anxiety, to contain it rather than letting it consume them. I'd like to suggest one way you might find helpful.

Instead of ruminating on a problem you can't solve, or catastrophizing about some terrible event or outcome that might happen, get out a sheet of paper and, at the top, write a brief statement of the problem. Then, draw a line down the middle of the page. On the left side, jot down all the bad events or outcomes that might occur ("I'll lose my job"). Next to each one, on the opposite side, write what you would do in response ("Call friends and colleagues to ask for contacts and leads").

Take your time with this and do it thoroughly, so the next time you begin to ruminate or catastrophize, you can read through what you've already reasoned out, with little or nothing to add. Since you've done the necessary contingency planning, this approach to problem analysis may substantially cut down on any fretting you might otherwise do. Some people find that, since they've already developed concrete plans of action, they no longer have to keep obsessing in the interest of coming up with them—they've already done the mental work.

I've used this approach to contingency planning. It works better than you might expect. Such planning is exceedingly hard to do when you're obsessing about bad things that might happen—when you're catastrophizing. Do it anyway.

PREDICTABILITY

Stable people are more or less predictable. Others know what to expect and are rarely if ever hit with disconcerting surprises. Others can therefore anticipate, in general, what a stable leader will say or do.

If a leader were totally predictable, so that everyone else knew *exactly* how he or she was going to act in every circumstance, that person wouldn't be much of a leader. What good would it do for a completely predictable leader even to show up for work? A robot might just as well run things. A leader's degree of predictability, therefore, has to be high, but not so high as to render that leader incapable of coming up with the occasional surprise. The late French president Charles de Gaulle may have been on to something when he quipped, "A true leader always keeps an element of surprise up his sleeve, which others can't grasp but which keeps his public excited and breathless."

What may be surprising to this public may, in fact, have been well thought out in advance and therefore reflect anything but instability. I vividly recall how much the future bride in a wedding I was asked to perform wanted it to be spontaneous. That was the last thing I wanted, since I knew that a spontaneous wedding would almost certainly mean a disorganized if not chaotic one. But I also knew that a well-planned wedding could *appear* spontaneous. If great art is to make it look easy, good leadership is to make the carefully orchestrated look like the smoothly casual. Fortunately, she quickly understood this, so together we set about planning the format of her wedding in detail.

When the big day arrived, the event came off flawlessly. Her father and stepfather walked her down the aisle to upbeat music, skipping as they went, and all elements of the ceremony blended together perfectly. The skipping itself was not planned, however, which demonstrates how constructive innovation will often emerge from a well-planned and executed structure—from a stable base. Innovations, which are often unplanned and unanticipated, sometimes alter the course of entire industries.

Undisciplined surprises, on the contrary, can prove dysfunctional, disruptive, and sometimes disastrous.

As a result of this experience, a sign now hangs on my office wall: "It's never spontaneous unless you plan it." This, of course, is an oxymoron, a self-contradiction, but it does emphasize the importance of forethought when it comes to the unexpected and of stability as the scaffolding for creativity.

CONVEYING STABILITY BY TRUSTING OTHERS

It's important for a leader to give others the benefit of the doubt, rather than imposing on them the burden of proof. He or she needs to operate according to the American judicial presumption, innocent until proven guilty, rather than the French one, guilty until proven innocent. We automatically tend to give those we trust the benefit of the doubt.

All of us are to some extent watchful if not wary. Without realizing it, we constantly scan our environments for danger. The instinctive vigilance that often accompanies working in an organization can sometimes lead otherwise trusting people to become unnecessarily guarded; this hardly suggests stability. It is best, therefore, to err on the side of trust. This does not mean being naive. Once someone demonstrates that he or she is unworthy of trust, keep a watchful eye. But trust as much as you can, for this communicates steadiness, and steadiness is the bedrock on which trust is erected.

Your subordinates, peers, and supervisors will tend to give you the benefit of the doubt to the extent that they view you as mature. They will also tend to trust you if they see that you trust them, if you empower them. Empowerment can be thought of as *demonstrated trust.*

COMMON COLDS AFFLICTING LEADERS

Although this is not a psychology textbook, I want to discuss several of the more common emotional difficulties that nearly all of us, including executives, suffer from now and then. These are normal if they do not become pronounced or prolonged, since just about everyone occasionally experiences them.

Anxiety and fear: There's a technical difference between anxiety and fear. Anxiety is free-floating and generalized, whereas fear is focused on a concrete object or specific outcome. It is sometimes assumed that people in high places live without anxiety or fear, but this is not so. No amount of status or money protects a person from either one. We all have periods of uneasiness, moments of dread, episodes of foreboding, times of silent panic, and at least a few seconds of outright terror. If nothing else, we may worry about going to the doctor and finding out we have an unexpected health problem.

The wise leader is discerning about what and to whom to communicate such emotions. We all need friends and confidants, those with whom we can and do share our private experiences. But, if you are a leader, you have a role to play, and this role requires you almost always to maintain what the British call a stiff upper lip. There may be times when you openly share aspects of your personal life, for example when you suffer a death in the family. But, it is best to keep most of your everyday anxieties and fears to yourself. Showing your vulnerability may let others see that you're human, and therefore increase your effectiveness as a leader, but you have to balance this with the role prescriptions you implicitly accept when you agree to become one.

As a leader, you stand *in loco parentis* to those in your charge. You function as a parent, which is how they will tend to regard you. This is true even for subordinates who are considerably older. It is natural for all of us to relate to those above us *as if* they were de facto parents, which doesn't make us wimps or weaklings. In fact, if a subordinate is unwilling to grant you this status, at least within the bounds of the organization's activities, he or she may turn out to be a problem.

Every moment you're with other people, you are training them in how to see and act toward you, and they are training you. We hardly realize this is going on, but it is. As the leader, it is not wise to train others to view you as inordinately troubled. The message, instead, should be that you can and will competently handle whatever comes at you.

Depression: There are many reasons why people become depressed. Some have a biological disposition toward depression, although such dispositions may be less common than is commonly assumed. Depression can result from feeling trapped, with no obvious way out. Sometimes people become depressed by turning their anger on themselves, often because they fear the consequences of directing it outwardly. There is also the phenomenon of adrenaline rebound. Coping with prolonged stress, such as a person would have to do in war, requires our bodies to produce extra adrenaline over a prolonged period. Once such stress is over, our bodies seem to compensate for this extra production either by underproducing adrenaline or becoming less sensitive to it, which in turn can cause us to become lethargic and depressed. Finally, depression nearly always accompanies loss.

Even a positive change can cause a person to become depressed, because most kinds of change involve at least some loss. Here is the usual progression:

$$Change \rightarrow Loss \rightarrow Depression$$

This in itself is normal.

Guilt: There is an odd feature to guilt. When people say they feel guilty, what's often going on unconsciously is that they expect to be punished. Unless you are a sociopath, you probably feel guilty about at least a few things you've done or failed to do, and not all of this may be because you expect divine or human retribution. Still, the next time you begin to feel guilty, ask yourself if you aren't worried that something bad is going to happen to you.

If guilt doesn't become too intense or chronic, it's probably nothing to worry about. It's a normal part of life. But if you become preoccupied with it, talk with a psychological professional about it.

Mood swings: Oscillations in your moods are also normal if they are not too pronounced. If, however, you find yourself feeling cheerful one day and for no apparent reason melancholic the next, there may be something wrong. Returning to the topic of depression, it has long been recognized that there are two general types of depression: *endogenous* and *exogenous.* Exogenous depressions are reactive or situational. Someone dies or you lose money. Endogenous depressions, on the other hand, are thought to have a substantial biological basis, as do unexplained bouts of pronounced euphoria, or alternations between the two. If you have wide mood swings that cannot be explained by what's happening in your life, it would probably be wise to consult a physician or a psychologist.

Anger: Some people are volatile and others placid. When you vent your anger on someone else, you will almost always pay a social price, and an important rule for living is to pay no unnecessary social prices. Don't give others a reason for payback. We will revisit this principle in Chapters 8 and 12. Angry outbursts, especially at work, are a signal that something is wrong. If you comfort yourself with statements like "this will never happen again," especially if it's happened more than once, you're probably denying the obvious—there's something going on inside of you that needs attention.

Negativism: Human beings vary enormously in their levels of optimism. Some people make lemonade out of lemons while others turn wine into vinegar. Although chronic negativism may not seem to be a form of instability, it sometimes reflects an underlying medical or psychological condition. Negativism can prove disruptive in an organization, if for no other reason than that it decreases morale. In a leader, negativity typically comes across as uninspiring pessimism fueled by hopelessness. Leaders need to show how the difficult, if not the seemingly impossible, can be done. Rather than coming up with or accepting reasons for *why not,* they need constantly to press for answers to the question *how.*

GETTING HELP WHEN YOU NEED IT

You don't have to be sick to get better. Almost everyone suffers now and then from anxiety, fear, depression, guilt, anger, and negativism; many if not most people have even thought at least once or twice in their lives about suicide. This is the common experience of humankind. There is a point, however, at which you should consider talking to a mental health professional, so I want to offer a few guidelines to help you determine when you've reached that point.

Guideline # 1: The common colds discussed earlier can all derail you, so if you find yourself troubled by any of them for long, seek the advice of an appropriate professional. Physicians and psychologists are obligated to honor your confidence.

Guideline # 2: As many people move through middle age and into the years when they can see a movie at a discount, alcohol intake tends to increase. The easiest way to determine if drinking is a problem is to ask this question: Do you or anyone around you believe you have a drinking problem—that you drink too much? For problem drinkers, denial is part of the disease, which is why the second part of this question is important. When it comes to alcohol intake, the ratchet only turns one way. The more and longer you drink, the more tolerance you develop.

I do not recommend psychotherapy or counseling alone as a way to address a drinking problem. There are inpatient treatment programs that work well and can be trusted to be discrete. Alcoholics Anonymous (AA) is an effective nonmedical option for many people. Notice that except in reference to AA, I have avoided the term *alcoholic.* This is because that word sometimes discourages people from getting help, which is also the case with the related term *alcoholism.* Because controversy continues over when and when not to label someone an alcoholic, this is not a useful term, and like alcoholism it can be used pejoratively. The one advantage for using either of them is that, as in AA, it prevents a person from slipping and sliding—he or she has to own the problem.

Guideline # 3: Nearly everything in the above guideline applies to other forms of substance abuse. I am almost certain that one manager I know lost his job because of cocaine ingestion. He was very thin and decidedly hyperactive, to the point that his judgment was seriously impaired. No matter what the particular substance, my recommendation is always going to be the same. Get help before you become a statistic. I would offer the same advice to anyone with a gambling problem because compulsive gambling wreaks havoc each year on many thousands of lives—and not just the gambler's.

Guideline # 4: If you've recently suffered the loss of someone close to you, it might make sense to talk with a specialist in loss and grieving. Not everyone needs to do this, but sometimes even a session or two can make a difference. If your organization has an employee assistance program (EAP), using it might be the easiest and least expensive way to connect with such a professional.

Guideline # 5: Finally, if you're having serious domestic trouble, find a professional with whom you can talk. Divorce or even separation can be among the most stressful events in a person's life, so if you're going through either one, it's important to make sure your performance at work does not visibly fall off. Getting the right support is important. See the Appendix for recommendations on how to find a therapist or counselor.

RECOMMENDATIONS FOR HANDLING PERSONAL PROBLEMS OF SUBORDINATES

As a leader, your concern and appreciation for a subordinate can unwittingly draw you into a position that can make it difficult to fulfill your primary leadership duties. These duties are to make your expectations clear, confirm that these expectations have been understood, provide periodic feedback on how well they are being met, document performance, and try to ensure that outcomes, such as salary increases and promotions, are commensurate with that performance. Although you also have a duty to coach and develop subordinates, this is secondary to your principal responsibility, which is to lead.

When you become aware that a subordinate, whether an employee or volunteer, is not meeting your expectations *and* this is because of a personal problem, you may be tempted to move into the role of confidant. You might be concerned, for example, that the subordinate is depressed. Or, while providing constructive feedback—a far better term than criticism—you might learn that a spouse has filed for divorce, is having an affair, or both. Perhaps the person just found out that a grown child is using drugs or has been arrested. Or, there might be someone issuing threats of bodily harm, perhaps an ex-husband. Any of these circumstances, and many more, could cause you to drift into the role of ongoing sympathetic listener and emotional caretaker.

Part of the allure of becoming such a listener and caregiver is that doing so can be affirming and gratifying. It's wonderful to be trusted and to have another person confide in you. By giving in to this temptation, however, you can compromise your ability to do your job. You cannot be a sympathetic confidant with its implied duty to accept a person as is, and also be the one to uphold performance standards, and, when necessary, provide corrective feedback and perhaps take disciplinary action. Functioning as both leader and confidant puts you in a dual-role relationship. These are generally to be avoided because they can bring with them competing duties that compromise objectivity.

I have seen more than a few leaders become mired in anguish because they did not anticipate the consternation that playing both roles would generate. What do you do when a subordinate has entrusted you with deep secrets and formed a strong attachment to you, possibly even coming to view you as the *only* person who truly understands, but who continues to perform poorly? How do you balance this additional self-created duty with your duty to the organization?

This is not to recommend becoming hard-hearted, or looking the other way when it is obvious that subordinates are having problems outside of work. By all means, listen to whatever they want to share, and provide reasonable assistance, perhaps by helping to connect them with whatever supportive resources your organization routinely authorizes, such as an EAP if it has one. But, let it remain your subordinates' responsibility to make use of these resources. Do not substitute yourself for them.

Your job is to lead with the attendant duty of making your expectations clear. And, your subordinate's job is to live up to your expectations and the organization's standards of performance. Beware of subtly redefining or complicating your job or beclouding your subordinate's responsibilities.

SIX

Conscientiousness: Initiative and Goal-Directedness

Do you get results and do you set goals that require you to stretch? How often do you proactively anticipate opportunities and challenges, and figure out what to do ahead of time, rather than merely reacting when they are on your doorstep? Is your level of energy high, or does it wax and wane? Are you diligent, reliable, and dependable, someone who comes through and delivers? Can you maintain focus rather than allowing yourself to get sidetracked?

Motivation is not always noble. It can be rooted in greed, arrogance, predation, or a hundred other less than admirable characteristics. More than a few leaders, for example, have wasted a lot of other people's time and energy because they were motivated to leave what they self-servingly called a legacy. Often, the longed-for legacy amounted to little more than a costly monument to pride.

In this book, I occasionally use the terms *motivation* and *conscientiousness* interchangeably. Keep in mind that this presumes the motivation to be positive. I have chosen to use conscientiousness for the title of this chapter to emphasize the importance of diligence, responsibility, and accountability.

Few leaders fail because they lack motivation. But, insufficient motivation prevents many of them from getting promoted. Organizations are typically structured as pyramids. There are far more lieutenants than generals and managers than executives. As a person moves up the pyramid, advancement becomes increasingly competitive.

The difference between a leader selected for promotion and one not selected is often a willingness to work harder. To advance, one usually has to be perceived as intelligent (Chapter 4), mature (Chapter 5), collaborative (Chapter 7), and flexible (Chapter 8). Strength in one of these areas can partly compensate for weakness in another. Comparatively few people get promoted, however, unless they have demonstrated the willingness to stay a little later, work a few more weekends, and make beyond-the-call-of-duty sacrifices.

I am not suggesting that this is how the world should work, only that this is how it *does* work. As much as organizations like to talk the language of work–life balance, not many reward people for choosing the personal side of the equation, especially when something important to the enterprise is at stake. There are a few exceptions. Because of family obligations, the chief financial officer for one best-of-class organization often comes to work at 9:30. She is enormously competent, works as hard if not harder than anyone except perhaps the CEO, and does not usually leave work until after 7:00. Still, in many organizations, no matter how late she stayed or how well she did his job, showing up after 8:00 or 8:30 would put her in jeopardy. At very least, she'd be on the suspect list. This is not necessarily a credit to these organizations—but it is a reality.

In a discussion I recently had with a director-level manager who'd been born and raised in Germany, I noted how although his country of origin is the most productive in Europe, many managers leave for their sports or social clubs around 4:00 P.M. The typical American manager, by contrast, is expected to leave no earlier than 5:00 or 6:00. He remarked that American corporations have what he termed a *presence* culture, whereas German companies have a *productivity* culture. As long as a worker is productive in Germany, there is no requirement to have backside-in-chair nine or ten hours a day.

Although it might be desirable for the United States to move a bit in the direction of Germany, the high levels of productivity that have epitomized America may, in no small way, be attributable to its at-your-desk ethos. Reckoning with reality, as opposed to deluding ourselves, it's important to acknowledge that many people who work for organizations in the United States are more likely to be perceived as industrious and high-potential if they are more rather than less often physically present.

A SUCCESS STORY

I have known the CEO of a Fortune 500 company for almost thirty years, from when she was in her late twenties. And, I have watched her move many times from job to job. Not all of these moves were to her liking. Regardless of her personal sentiments, she did each one with excellence. When she was in her early thirties, the vice president to whom she reported told me she had given him twenty-eight objectives for the coming year. Her peers had each turned in far fewer. I generally advise managers to focus on a relatively small number of objectives so they don't lose focus, but she managed to achieve all twenty-eight because she worked so hard. This is the kind of motivation that underlies superior corporate achievement.

Some people hide behind a flurry of activity. They look motivated, but in reality what onlookers may mistake for motivation is but poorly channeled drive. The difference between drive and motivation is that drive only becomes motivation when it is directed toward a goal. I once saw a sign on the desk of the chief operating officer of a large bank: *Never confuse effort with results.* Indeed!

EXCEEDING THE THRESHOLDS

For every level in any organization, a person has to demonstrate a certain amount of conscientiousness to reach it. The amount needed to reach a particular level, such as director, commander, or vice president, differs from organization to organization. Since there is no simple way to measure conscientiousness, it's impossible to tell with precision what these requirements are. Still, they exist and operate as thresholds you should try to exceed if you aspire to ascend. How well people above you believe you do this will almost certainly affect your advancement.

It's a good idea to determine, as best you can, if you have the motivation to advance. Are you willing to stay later, work weekends, and make sacrifices? If you decide for whatever reason you aren't, make peace with this. I have seen managers caught in the neurotic bind of wanting contradictory things. They desired to advance but were unwilling to do what was necessary. I have also seen some who openly declared they didn't want to be considered for promotion because spending time with their families was more important to them than additional money or status.

CONSCIENTIOUSNESS AND TRUST

Your level of conscientiousness heavily influences how others evaluate both your competence and character. The harder you work at anything, especially over a long period of time, the better you become at it. So, it is almost inevitable that a high level of sustained motivation will make you more competent. And, as others see you work hard toward goals they consider worthwhile, they will also come to regard you as more ethical. Motives reflect values. People will infer your values from your motives, and your motives from your actions. Here's the causal chain:

$$Values \rightarrow Motives \rightarrow Actions$$

Reasoning backward, from actions through motives to values, others will draw conclusions about your values, and by implication about your character, based on what they see you do. They will form opinions about your habits of the heart, the title of a book from the 1980s. If you act for the right reasons, those around you will usually realize this. If you act for the wrong reasons, they will realize this too.

These, then, are the sorts of questions you should ask yourself: How much do others trust you to get things done? Will you walk through walls when that's the only way to move the enterprise ahead? And, perhaps most important of all in the end, do you care—about them, the organization, and society?

WAYS TO RUN OFF THE RAILS

I want to outline several stumbling blocks to success as a leader. There are more, of course, but these are the ones that sometimes derail careers.

Derailer # 1: Failing to close. Many years ago, my colleagues and I developed a Leadership Effectiveness Survey, an upward evaluation tool designed to provide organizations with information about the impact of leaders on subordinates. It yields scores in four domains: general leadership, informational leadership, relational leadership, and competitional leadership. We will return to these in Chapter 11. The most important of the four is the first one, general leadership. Among the items on which subordinates rate their leaders is, "Gets things done."

Some ineffective salespeople will tell you about a product for three hours, but never get around to asking you to buy it. They are insufficiently goal-directed. Nearly all successful people have the capacity to lock onto a target and stay locked on. If you don't know when to let go, of course, that's a problem. But, if you have little or no ability to hold on, you'll end up as your own worst enemy, sidelined because others won't be able to count on you. All of this has to do with persistence, thoroughness, following through, and the willingness to do whatever it takes. It also has to do with reliability and a deep sense of duty and responsibility.

Derailer # 2: Shoddiness. In 1942, the Provost Marshal General of the Army issued an important document that, three quarters of a century later, is still widely available on the Internet. Titled the *Doctrine of Completed Staff Work,* it is worth pondering, and perhaps also distributing to anyone who works for you. In the following summary of it, I have substituted a general term for one more specific to the military, *leader* for *chief,* changed *memoranda* to *e-mails* so it's more current, and loosened it slightly. I have also made a few other minor modifications so it's more pertinent to a wider range of readers. But I have not altered the essence of the document.

Its central idea is to take a problem from initial identification to final solution, such that the person to whom you report has only to indicate approval or disapproval. The more challenging the problem, the more you may be inclined to take it to your leader in bits and pieces. Completed staff work implies resisting this temptation whenever you can. It's your job to figure out the relevant elements of the problem, which may prove daunting, and to do this you may, and perhaps should, confer with peers and subordinates. But it is important to refrain from relying on your leader for help you can get elsewhere. What you develop, for example a new policy or recommended change to an existing one, should be in finished form. The *Doctrine* can serve as a powerful antidote to laziness.

Incomplete work is almost always shoddy work, which is why I am taking up the idea of completed staff work here. Shoddy work fosters upward delegation—shifting work onto a leader—and this can happen in a thousand ways, such as asking him or her to take a quick look at a draft you've written but not fully thought out. There's nothing wrong with asking the leader to look at a rough draft, as long as you've taken it as far as you can and it does not present an inadequately developed idea. But, such a draft must not become a vehicle for shifting responsibility onto the leader.

Concepts in the *Doctrine of Completed Staff Work* apply not only to someone whose job is officially designated *staff;* in relation to their leader(s), everyone is staff. If your boss has to redo your work, you haven't finished it. The *Doctrine* may seem to discourage collaboration between persons of different rank. Necessary collaboration is desirable, since it lessens the possibility of heading off in the wrong direction; unnecessary collaboration, on the contrary, merely chews up a leader's time.

The *Doctrine* points out that inexperienced managers may be subject to a fair amount of frustration, which makes them all the more inclined to depend on the leader. It counsels managers to resist such dependence: "It is your job to advise your leader what ought to be done, not to ask what you ought to do." It continues, "A leader needs answers, not questions." It is the subordinate's job to "study, write, restudy and rewrite" until he or she has developed, from among the alternatives, the best recommended action. We will explore the issue of recommending which action to take, versus reporting on one you've already taken, when we discuss empowerment in Chapter 15.

It is important not to subject the leader to long, tangential, or marginally relevant explanations or justifications. Get to the point. Think through the wisdom of any e-mail you want to send. This may create more work for you, but it creates less work for the leader. Sometimes, completed staff work results in a single document that requires only the leader's signature; if the leader wants comments or explanations, he or she will ask for them. Two salutary benefits of following the principles in the *Doctrine* are, first, it protects leaders from poorly reasoned ideas, ponderous e-mails, and rambling dialogues, and, second, by increasing efficiency it enables subordinates with good ideas more easily to promote them. The test of whether you have delivered completed staff work is to ask if you'd be willing to stake your professional reputation on what you've proposed. If your answer is *no,* "take it back and work it over, because it is not yet completed staff work."

Derailer # 3: Lack of initiative and energy. To demonstrate enough motivation to inspire trust, you have to think ahead. Such thinking takes effort. And, actually doing whatever you've decided to do takes even more. You have to show a certain amount of proactivity to succeed as a leader.

Some high-ranking executives have chauffeurs. I can still picture the face of one driver I was asked to coach. He would show up late for the executive he was assigned to drive, and when he finally appeared, he hadn't yet looked up the directions for how to get to their destination. This happened before GPS devices were in common use, and people were still using books of maps. He never did learn to look up the route in advance and was eventually replaced. I have seen failures at much higher levels for essentially the same reason: *failure to care enough to think ahead.*

There is little or no correlation between intelligence and how quickly someone talks. A person who speaks slowly may be highly intelligent, and someone who speaks rapidly may be almost entirely without cortical power. Those who enunciate slowly and say little in meetings, however, can come across as less than optimally motivated, having low energy, and lacking initiative. This may or may not be the reality, but the social perception is likely to be that slow speech or infrequent participation implies low motivation. Pay attention to your level of animation as reflected in how you talk. Too much animation, and you'll come across as hyperactive and unfocused. Too little, and those around you will wonder if you're about to fall asleep. In either case, they may not trust you to lead.

Derailer # 4: Inconsistency. A senior manager I know was never promoted. For years, I could make no sense of this, so I finally asked a senior executive why. Her response was, "he's inconsistent." If those above you perceive you as on-again/off-again, you will probably hit a plateau. They may not trust you enough to promote you above it. Your peers and subordinates might have doubts about your consistency as well.

Among the most important things you can do to get others to trust you is to be reliable. If you often call in sick or at the wrong time, or schedule your vacations when the organization is likely to face major challenges, you are not going to increase your trust quotient.

Derailer # 5: Diversion. The efforts of some leaders on behalf of the enterprise become diluted—like what happens to the value of shares when a publicly held company issues more stock. I have in mind those who contribute as little as they can or are involved in outside businesses. Effort can also become diluted by other kinds of choices, such as the decision to work from home, which may or may not make sense.

Those who slack off in their duties may have given up hope of ever being promoted, and they may have little fear of getting fired. Such behavior makes not getting promoted almost certain and immunity from termination uncertain. No one is going to trust a slacker to lead.

As for operating a business on the side, few people can keep this a secret. Unless you have a routine job in which you clock in and out and get paid for a set number of onsite hours, even needing to keep it a secret suggests that, by diluting your efforts in this way, you may be cheating your employer. There's an ethics issue here. Organizations value and reward loyalty and commitment.

TELECOMMUTING

I want briefly to discuss the troublesome issue of working from home or a substitute office—telecommunicating. Some jobs are more suited to this than others. If, for example, you're a manager overseeing five factories spread over a large geographic territory, you may have to do a lot of telecommunicating, to the point that you may do most of your work from home and out of your car. Sometimes, an organization simply cannot provide you with office space, in which case you will have to telecommute much of the time. It is still important to visit headquarters or the home office as often as you reasonably can.

Once you reach a certain level in any organization, telecommunicating is almost always a bad idea. This is because *out of sight, out of mind.* Again, we live and work in a presence culture. I know one man who was promoted to an executive position in part because, although he was assigned to run an international satellite business and therefore lived in another country, he visited the mother ship often enough to ensure that he was not forgotten.

In addition to enhancing your chances of promotion, another reason for regularly going into the office is that, by doing so, you're more likely to be in the know and part of the action. Psychologists sometimes talk about *response availability,* by which they mean how easy it is to retrieve information or activate a learned response stored in memory. The notion of response availability can easily be adapted to organizational life, where we might think of it as *participation availability.* If you're not there, you can't participate.

Aside from missing out on important information and not being able to participate, the two biggest reasons for *not* telecommunicating are, first, that working remotely causes you to lose the benefit of what psychologists call *social facilitation:* we tend to be more productive, whether at work or the gym, if we're around others who are productive. Second, telecommunicating brings with it the risk of becoming distracted. If you're going to work at home, or in a surrogate office such as the library, make sure you can do so without distraction. This is not to suggest that you choose work over family, but it is a candid recognition that, contrary to popular mythology, you cannot always have it all—you can't do everything, certainly not at the same time. You have only so much time and energy, and because we are finite creatures with limitations, nearly every choice we make brings with it what economists call *opportunity costs*—selecting option A often makes it impossible also to select option B, C, and D.

THREE RULES FOR LIVING

Framed and posted on my office wall is a set of rules for living. Several relate directly or indirectly to motivation. Rule # 3 is, *Always have a Plan B.* The goal is to accomplish the mission, whatever that is; only the foolish are willing to have in mind only one way to do this.

This rule flows out of Rule # 2, *You have to care.* This is because, if you care enough, you will probably think ahead and have a backup plan. You have to *want* to accomplish the mission.

Rule # 1 is, *It can be done.* You have to believe in yourself and your team. Caring, together with contingency planning, facilitates optimism, and it is from such optimism that a person comes to believe that the seemingly impossible may become the already achieved.

INTEGRITY

Note that the word *conscientious* is related to *conscience.* It may come as no surprise, therefore, that conscientious leaders are by definition people of integrity; a principle that runs throughout this book is its emphasis on character. Among the dimensions of the Big Five, this one most directly bears on and reflects good character.

As noted in the opening section of this chapter, I have chosen to view motivation as a virtue. It must be conceded, however, that people can be driven to do many things that are anything but virtuous. Acquisitiveness or ambition clearly seduces some to wander over the ethical or legal lines. Fortunately, in a society like ours, in which duty to society customarily trumps duty to tribe or clan, there is *comparatively* little corruption. Organizations in the highly developed Western world generally operate differently than those in some other parts of the globe where, when you get a job, your first duty is to make sure your brother and cousin get one too.

As long as you don't fall into the trap of thinking of the following term as an anatomical part, I would like to suggest that we each have within us an *integrity module.* Those who are highly conscientious have a well-developed one. Make sure you're counted among them.

SEVEN

Friendliness: Collegiality and Collaboration

Can you establish and maintain long-term collaborative relationships—are you able to build friendships and alliances? Do you have a reputation for honest and straightforward dealings, in contrast to manipulative, angular, or treacherous ones? How often do you move toward others, rather than against or away from them? Are you known for loyalty and steadfast support?

The word *collegial* is closely related to *colleague.* To relate to others collegially, therefore, is to treat them as colleagues. It is to interact with them as *friends,* to move toward rather than against or away from them, and to care about their welfare. Reduced to essentials, to be collegial is to collaborate and engage in mutual support. Leaders do not always fail because they lack ability or motivation. One frequent cause of failure, as we have seen, is instability. Another is that leaders may find themselves sabotaged or frozen out.

When the cause is sabotage, it is often because the leader has been so nasty that others actively look for ways to undermine the leader's success. Sabotage can take passive forms, such as failing to protect a leader ("Chris is *still* at lunch"), repeating malicious rumors ("Jordan is sleeping with Morgan"), or badmouthing the leader to senior management ("I don't think we can trust Corey to come through"). Or, it can be more active, such as calling in an anonymous but false complaint on the organization's hotline ("Jean is misappropriating company property") or intentionally giving the leader misleading information ("The meeting's at headquarters," when it's at a regional office).

Sabotage can even take overtly aggressive forms, such as deflating or puncturing tires or pouring glue over the papers on your desk; it can also escalate into overt pushing and shoving. Extreme forms of opposition seldom occur among leaders in a corporate context, but if some people become sufficiently angry, they will resort to almost anything. Early in my consulting career, I knew an engineer who so enraged subordinates that, while he was inspecting their underground work, they threw a rattlesnake down the manhole through which he had descended. Although he managed to avoid the snake, the experience was, to say the least, decidedly unnerving.

Failure can also result from being frozen out. If this ever happens to you, it is probably not so much that anyone is deliberately trying to do you in but that they simply refuse to include you. If you experience enough exclusion, you may become so demoralized that you resign. For others to include you in a meeting or even to share information, you usually have to enjoy their goodwill. If you've repeatedly given them reasons to shun or ignore you, it's only a matter of time before your career in that organization will, in some way or another, come to an end.

As just one example of how this can happen, I knew an executive who was smart, had good executive presence, and came with plenty of relevant experience. But my first impression was that he appeared arrogant, was not a good listener, and could be dismissive. He was eager to tell me how superior he was to his professional peers; he would interrupt in mid-sentence when I was trying to share something I believed would be of value to him; and, he seemed to trivialize the feedback and coaching I gave him ("I already know that, and it's not important anyway"). It wasn't that he and I failed to get on well. I sincerely liked him and he seemed to like me. It seemed clear from the beginning that he was going to have a hard time gaining traction.

I typically spend a day a month at each of my client organizations, and any executive or senior-level manager can sign up for time. Within a few months of joining the company, he got on the calendar for my monthly visit. He came to see me because he was not receiving invitations to meetings he believed he should attend. Worse, he knew he could add value. And, he was right. This man was impressively knowledgeable and, in some areas, had more experience than anyone else in the company. When I asked around, I was told, yes, he definitely had something to contribute, but getting it was not worth putting up with his posture of superiority. The pain of exclusion eventually became so intense that he resigned. I'm not sure if he ever figured out why he'd so often failed to make the guest list.

BUILDING MULTIPLE CONSTITUENCIES

When I first started consulting, an experienced organizational psychologist told me, "You have to build multiple constituencies—up, down, and sideways." By this he meant get as many people voting for you as possible, since you can never predict with certainty when the support of any one of them may be important. How you stand with your peers, for example, can make a lot of difference, if for no other reason than that one of them may later turn out to be your boss.

Even the parking attendant may be helpful, if for example you're late for a career-determining meeting and have to ask the attendant to park your car, especially if this is not customary practice. Those few extra minutes could make or break you. I've made it a point to treat executive and administrative assistants with special respect, in part because I appreciate what they do and how hard they work. I have often thought that, just as nurses run hospitals, executive and administrative assistants run corporations; they make everything run smoothly. But I also treat them well because I live or die by their support or lack thereof.

CHOOSING BATTLES AND FORMING ALLIANCES

There will, of course, be times when no matter what you do, you're going to end up in conflict with someone else. Going to war if you know you're going to lose is unwise. Yet, many people do precisely that. Sometimes they'll tell you it was a matter of principle, and I have no doubt they believe this. I recognize there are times when, regardless of probable outcome, it's important to take a stand—it *is* a matter of principle. Such a claim, however, often serves as a self-comforting excuse for poor judgment. Choose your battles wisely.

When you have to go into battle, it's important to have allies. You won't have them if you've never entered into alliances. An example of forming alliances is establishing rapport individually with participants before a meeting, which is always a good idea, especially if you've never met them and the outcome of the meeting is important. And, as Dennis Arriola once pointed out to me, it's not the best time to introduce yourself when you're about to ask for a favor. Make the connection beforehand if you can. Just be wise about all this, since you only have so much discretionary time. If choosing your battles is important, choosing your allies is even more important.

UNDERSTANDING HOW PEOPLE ACT

Grasping how people shape each other's behavior can prove useful, so I want to summarize four principles that undergird such shaping. These principles have been well supported by decades of research. It would require more space than we have to explore them in detail, but we can at least outline them. The material in this section may take a bit of work to assimilate, but I urge you to expend the effort needed to master it. It will enable you to understand how and why people behave as they do in a wide variety of contexts.

I am using the adjectives *social* and *interpersonal* interchangeably. Both refer to what a person does in the presence of one or more other people, whether talking in the hall or chatting at a party. Person A says or does something, to which Person B responds. Person A then reacts to what B just said or did, and so on. Just about any conversation between two or more people conforms to this kind of alternating pattern.

Principle #1: All interpersonal behavior reflects some combination of friendliness and assertiveness. What each person says or does in a social setting suggests some measure of friendliness and some measure of assertion. These are the last two components of the Big Five (we will take up assertiveness in Chapter 8). Remember that, like all dimensions of the five-factor model, these two are independent of each other. They do not cause each other, nor can they be predicted from each other. It makes sense, therefore, to think of them as two axes, one running north and south (assertiveness), and the other running east and west (friendliness).

We can easily come up with labels for each of the four quadrants created by crossing these two axes (dimensions). The labels in the diagram will do for our purposes.

If we combine (cross) high assertiveness with high friendliness, we end up with *friendly assertion* (FA). This is what people ordinarily mean by extraversion. If we combine high assertiveness with low friendliness, we have *hostile assertion* (HA). Combining high friendliness and low assertiveness gives us *friendly compliance* (FC), a kind of benevolent support. And, putting low friendliness and low assertiveness together yields *hostile compliance* (HC). Anything anyone says or does in relation to another person can be mapped onto this diagram. Study any television drama with it in your hand and you'll quickly see that this is so.

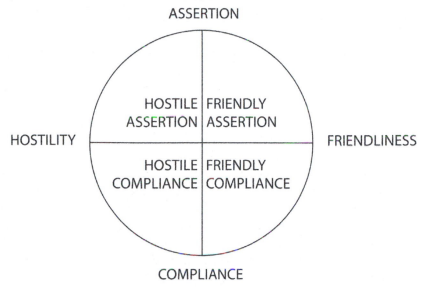

Figure 7.1   Dimensions of Interpersonal Relationships

Principle #2: When you interact with another person, you are teaching that person how to treat you—and he or she is teaching you. Such mutual training almost always takes place more or less unconsciously. Neither person is aware of it. We alluded to it in Chapter 5.

Suppose Doug and his wife Linda come to our house for dinner. Linda and my wife Anna embrace (FA), and Doug and I shake hands (FA). When we move into the dining room, I say, "Doug, sit here" (FA). He smiles, I smile back, and he takes his seat (FC). Doug and Linda are obviously pleased that we have invited them, and we are just as pleased they were able to accept our invitation. What, we might ask, has happened so far?

When Doug and Linda walked through the door, we were warm to them, and they were warm in return. Our warmth invited and reinforced their warmth. When I pointed to a particular seat, Doug knew that I was continuing my friendly stance, but *he also knew that I was gently directing him.* If I were in his home, he would have directed me in a similar fashion. And, as he did tonight, I would have accepted his direction. Training does not always require words. Sometimes, a smile and a gesture will do.

This vignette depicts a healthy social interchange. It narrates what people typically do, and the sort of reactions they *pull* from each other. We made the social overture of answering the door and warmly inviting our friends in (FA), and they returned our overture with warm acceptance (FC).

They could have said, "Why would we want to join *you* for dinner? We can't stand either of you, and we expect any meal you serve to be terrible" (HA). When I invited Doug to sit at the table facing me, implying that Anna and Linda also sit across from each other, he could have said, "I don't want to sit *there*. I want to sit facing Linda" (more HA). This is not how normal people act, or how social behavior ordinarily works. Such reactions are highly irregular in polite society.

Principle #3: People tend to match each other on friendliness, and to complement[1] each other on assertiveness. If the other person is friendly, we tend to be friendly in return. If, on the contrary, the other person is nasty, our reflex is to return the nastiness. People do not always give in to the impulse to return aggression or hostility in kind. But, unless they are under duress and therefore have a motive to fake collegiality, relatively few will continue to act warmly toward someone who abuses them. Friendly people seek out other friendly people with whom to associate. And, hostile or aggressive people also manage to find each other.

As suggested in the first paragraph of this chapter, there are three ways people can orient themselves toward other people: toward, against, or away. Unless you have a compelling reason to do otherwise, it is advisable to move *toward,* which is especially important when the other person has turned hostile or is starting to freeze you out. This is also when moving toward may prove the most difficult.

Moving *against* is just what it sounds like—aggression—while moving *away* amounts to withdrawal. If you are dealing with a seriously disturbed person, this is sometimes the wisest course to follow. Otherwise, move toward and move toward some more, so that you nip in the bud any festering mistrust.

On the east–west axis, each person tends to mirror the other person's warmth or lack of it. On the north–south axis, however, it is a different story. People who are high on assertiveness generally induce others to be low on assertiveness—to act deferentially or compliantly. Dominant people train others to be submissive, and submissive people train others to be dominant. This is not always the case, of course, which is why many people end up in dominance struggles.

We noted earlier that friendly people look for friendly companions, and hostile people look for hostile companions. The same kind of pairing occurs with assertiveness, only the interpersonal pairing is reciprocal (complementary) rather than matching (mirroring). Assertive people seek out and find compliant people, and vice versa. People who act deferentially invite others to lead them, and those who act submissively invite others to dominate them.

Principle #4: Overtures and reinforcements operate north and south in the diagram. Overtures are invitations, bids for the other person to respond in a compatible way. Reinforcements in this context are whatever makes such compatible behavior more probable. This principle draws out the implications of Principle #3. Friendly assertion and friendly compliance invite and reinforce each other, while hostile assertion and hostile compliance invite and reinforce each other.

If, as an example from the left side of the diagram, one person scurries in the face of being bullied, the bullying will usually increase. Bullying is a kind of hostile assertion and scurrying is a kind of hostile compliance. Scurrying is saturated with resentment—suppressed and veiled aggression. This is why it belongs in the bottom left quadrant.

As an example from the right side, if one person acts with friendly compliance, the other person is naturally inclined to act with friendly assertion, with an attempt to lead. And, turning things around, if one person begins to enact friendly assertion, the other person naturally tends to respond with friendly compliance.

Such behavioral compatibility is by no means always the case. But once relationships reach equilibrium, they tend to operate according to these principles. In a healthy relationship, people remain friendly but take turns leading. One person may be good with words, and so will write the thank-you notes, while the other person may be good with spatial relations, and so will be the navigator when they're driving.

RELATIONAL TENSION

Two kinds of interpersonal patterns are out of equilibrium and will therefore tend to change. Consider, first, what happens if people relate diagonally in the diagram—if, for instance, one person behaves with friendly assertion and the other person responds with hostile compliance. Or, if one person acts with hostile assertion and the other friendly compliance. They have worked out their relationship on the assertiveness axis but have yet to work it out on the friendliness axis. The relationship is therefore out of balance. If they are to avoid chronic discord, they will either avoid each other, become mutually friendly, or turn mutually hostile.

Next, consider what happens if relationships follow an east–west pattern—if, for instance, one person behaves with hostile assertion and the other with friendly assertion. They are neither matching each other on collegiality, nor complementing each other on assertiveness. Such a relationship is markedly out of balance. If they are to remain in it and avoid perpetual tension, one of them will become more dominant. And beyond that, for the relationship to reach equilibrium, one also has to move to the other side of the diagram: either the hostile person will turn friendly, or the friendly person will turn hostile. Note that a relationship that has achieved equilibrium and is therefore resistant to change is *not* necessarily a healthy one. It may, in fact, be strikingly pathological.

Treating other people graciously usually prompts them to return your graciousness. This was an implication of Principle #3. A noteworthy downside of treating people poorly is that this gives them a reason for payback. When you need a favor, they will not be there, and if you overtly attack them, they may lie in wait to ambush you.

SERVANT LEADERSHIP

I'd like to highlight the virtues of acting graciously by appealing to what has come to be known as *servant leadership*. The basic idea is that if you want to be a leader, first become a servant. If you're interested in doing the best you can by and for others, you will almost inevitably influence them. Whether or not they realize it, you will probably lead them.

Robert K. Greenleaf coined the term *servant-leader,* which grew out of his long career with A.T.&T. When he worked there, it was by far the largest private sector employer in the world. He retired in 1964 as A.T.&T.'s director of management research. Before he died in 1990, he held a joint appointment as visiting lecturer at the MIT Sloan School of Management and the Harvard Business School, and he taught at both Dartmouth and the University of Virginia. Greenleaf also consulted for several nonprofits, including the Ford Foundation, the R.K. Mellon Foundation, and the Lilly Endowment.

In 1970, he published *The Servant as Leader,*[2] which numbered fewer than fifty pages. But it inspired an approach to leadership that has since been embraced by thousands of leaders. I want to emphasize that these leaders are by no means weak; many are by nature strong and forceful.

The opening words of Greenleaf's short book are, "Servant and Leader. Can these two roles be fused in one real person, [at] all levels of status or calling? If so, can that person live and be productive in the real world ... ?" He believed the answer to both questions was yes.

Greenleaf observed that the usual motif for a person in management is to try to scratch and claw up the organization, and then perhaps at the age of sixty, do something nice for the parking attendant. By this time, the successful businessperson certainly has the power to do it. But what in fact often happens is that, by this age, he or she has become so war weary and steeped in the ethos of ever-vigilant competition that the parking attendant has long been forgotten. The leader may also have lost touch with the so-called common man, and such sensitivty as he or she once had has been replaced by an elixir that calcifies the heart.

The idea of the servant as leader came to Greenleaf as a result of reading Hermann Hesse's *Journey to the East*. In that novella, a small group sets out on a journey. They engage a guide named Leo, a man of considerable presence who does their menial chores and generally sustains them. Everything goes swimmingly until Leo disappears, after which the expedition falls into disarray and the group abandons the quest. Years later, the narrator finds Leo, is received into the Order that had originally sponsored the journey, and discovers that Leo, whom he had known only as servant, is its titular head—"its guiding spirit, a great and noble *leader.*"

Robert Toms, who once served as Commissioner of the California Department of Corporations, introduced me to Greenleaf's writings. He also shared his personal philosophy of leadership, which has helped me considerably over the years: "Make the other guy the hero." Rather than rushing ahead or cutting in line, help the other person look good. I have since combined this advice with the Pittsburgh Steelers' motto, to formulate the watchword for my consulting practice: *Whatever it takes to help you do your best.*

I couldn't tell you how many bullet points I've written or how much behind-the-scenes planning I've done, but no one will ever know about any of this, at least not from me. If you do your best to help others do their best, someday when you least expect and perhaps most need it, they may return the favor.

PUTTING HOSTILITY ON EXTINCTION

Extinction is a concept that comes from the psychology of learning: If you don't reward a behavior, it will eventually drop out. If, to the contrary, you reward undesirable behavior by playing the good sport, it is likely to get worse.

I once made the mistake in a professional setting of allowing abusive behavior to go on far too long. This only intensified it. I should have put it on extinction by not reacting and ignoring it, rather than continuing to behave in the friendly way I did. When you respond to verbal hostility by *not* reacting, the other person usually ends up feeling awkward and foolish, which makes further hostility less likely. But you have to be consistent. If you lapse back into the role of the good sport, you will make it harder to stop the abuse than if you'd never put it on extinction in the first place.[3]

WHEN THE OTHER PERSON LACKS A CONSCIENCE

Some people have very well-developed consciences. If a vending machine delivers too much change, they try somehow to return it. Other people are almost completely without consciences. They are not just hostile, but ethically deficient and instinctively predatory; they are victimizers. They will not match your collegiality, not over the long haul, and they delight in finding someone on whom to take out their aggressions. The friendlier you act toward them, the weaker they conclude you are, and the more they try to make you squirm. As a general rule, the most pathological person in a relationship determines its nature.

Often, you will initially find such people interesting and charming. If you meet them at a party, they may enchant you because they can be colorful. When I taught college, I used to tell students that, if they encountered someone they instantly liked and found intriguing, "Watch out!" The person may be the perfect date and possibly the perfect mate, but he or she might also turn out to be a monster devoid of compassion. We'll return to the subject of compassion in Chapter 14.

Sociopathic people have underdeveloped consciences. Many of society's less gifted sociopaths end up in prison. They flagrantly trample on the rights of others and have little regard for person or property. If, however, they have been well educated and raised in an affluent family, they may be less driven to flout the law and less overtly violent. And, so, we might describe them as sociopathic but not outright sociopaths. Still, the damage they do can be far greater than that done by the career burglar or car thief. Think of all the financial harm inflicted on individuals and society by a relatively small cadre of sociopathic investment fund managers.

When people with defective consciences find their way into organizations, they are usually identified sooner or later and treated like viruses—organizational antibodies wage war against them. They may do well for a while, but their predation eventually catches up with them, at which point they may move to another organization where, once again, they become predatory. Since, to avoid liability, a past employer will usually provide only previous dates of employment, sociopathic managers can often start anew each time they move to a new job.

One smart, engaging, but ethically deficient manager used to work for one of my client companies. To look more successful, he made many promises on its behalf that simply could not be fulfilled. But, this didn't matter, at least not to him. He was off to another enterprise, leaving the company to bear the considerable ill will of those to whom he'd made the promises.

The most common reason sociopathic leaders fail is that others learn not to trust them. Some prove to be ruthless competitors who will stop at nothing to win their next bonus, raise, or promotion. Others turn out to have fraudulent credentials. Still others betray confidences for personal advantage, turn out to be chronic liars, or are discovered to be crafty embezzlers. Sooner or later, they alienate nearly everyone around them. Many end up getting fired, wearing handcuffs, or both.

Years ago, I facilitated a daylong succession-planning meeting attended by a company's executives. Just before the noon break, one of them made some vague but unfavorable comments about a senior manager. Although I didn't know the manager well, he seemed like a nice enough fellow. He had graduated from an Ivy League college, served in the Special Forces, and was an expert on wine—impressive!

During the break, I approached the executive. "What you said in there may have ruined his chances of getting promoted." This executive had been around and was a good judge of horseflesh. "There's something about him that's not quite right, Mac," he replied. "I don't know what it is, but it's there." I'd already learned to take his opinions seriously. Still, it seemed he'd been unduly harsh.

Months later, the manager was caught inflating his expense report. Then the company discovered that he'd been involved in what looked suspiciously like embezzlement. When they checked further into his background, they found out, to their horror and chagrin, that he'd never attended college. Nor had he served in the military. He'd falsified both his educational transcript and military record. As for his oenological expertise, that, too, may have been trumped up. The company quietly let him go. A year or two later, he was arrested in another state for financial impropriety. His new employer was less reluctant to prosecute, and he was sentenced to several years in prison.

Sociopathic people are superb at *establishing* relationships—they appear to bond quickly—but they are lousy at *maintaining* them. What appears to be instant bonding turns out later to have been an illusion, a by-product of manipulative pretense and the compulsive need to take advantage of others. Rather than establishing person-to-person relationships, they create predator-to-prey ones. Sociopaths don't do things with you. They do things *to* you.

MENTAL DISTURBANCE AND AGGRESSION

We noted in Chapter 3 that the usual lack of predictability between and among the components of the Big Five operates for normal people, but not always for the seriously disturbed. It may not be immediately apparent that an individual is psychiatrically impaired. Some people appear normal and work productively, but they turn out to be capable of severely aggressive conduct. They can seem put-together one moment and flagrantly deranged the next—they quickly but briefly decompensate into a psychotic-like state and, just as quickly, pull themselves together.

There is a correlation between hostility and psychosis, which we will define as a mental disorder in which the person is grossly out of touch with reality. A psychotic individual has bizarre thoughts and behaves in abnormal ways. The more hostile a person, the more he or she is likely to have such thoughts and do such things. If the psychosis includes the delusion that other people are dangerous and potentially harmful, that alone is enough to trigger assaultive behavior: if others are out to hurt you, one strategy is to hurt them first. Most psychotic people are not dangerous. But there are exceptions.

In the film *Fatal Attraction,* Manhattan attorney Dan (Michael Douglas) meets attractive publishing company editor Alexandra (Glenn Close). While his wife and daughter are away for the weekend, Dan and Alex have a torrid affair. After he announces that he has to go home, she cuts her wrists, begins to stalk him, visits his wife under false pretenses, kidnaps their daughter, pours acid on his car, murders the daughter's pet rabbit, and boils it in a pot on their stove. These sorts of things do happen. Such people exist. They are not the invention of Hollywood. Fortunately, they are exceedingly rare.

Every one of us falls somewhere on a continuum from being fully in touch with reality to entirely out of touch, living in a world of illusion. Otherwise normal looking people can occasionally surprise you. They do not hallucinate, nor do they believe the CIA or mafia is out to get them. But they are in subtle ways a bit crazy, and so, without notice, they may turn nasty. I have not written this section to scare but rather to warn you. Keep your eyes open and do not play into the pathology of a seriously disturbed person if and when you encounter one. This *is* the time to move away, rather than toward or against. The good news is that you will rarely encounter them above the first-line supervisor level. Their bizarre behavior typically surfaces early enough to prevent them from getting promoted.

SELF-DEFEATING NARCISSISM

Narcissism is self-absorption, usually accompanied by the narcissist trying to demonstrate how smart, attractive, or virtuous he or she is. The social effect of such attention seeking is that other people end up feeling stupid, ugly, or inadequate—and angry. Narcissistic people bolster their self-esteem by putting others down and making them feel defective. Contrary to appearances, the narcissist suffers from low self-esteem. They are often oblivious to the amount of hostility they generate in those around them. Even if they are aware of it, their need to one-up others is, like the sociopath's need for predation, compulsive. They can't help it.

I knew a talented executive who almost got himself fired because of such narcissistic displays. By any measure, he was smart. He was also the most creative person in the software company for which he worked. But he incessantly told others how intelligent he was, and by implication how dim-witted they were.

FATAL LITERALISM

Executives and managers, when they are hired from outside an organization, are sometimes told by senior executives, "We want you to be an agent of change, to shake things up around here." Such utterances reflect no intent to deceive, but they omit an important but unspoken clause: *within the limits of the organization's tolerance.*

I have seen executives and managers fail because, in taking such spoken words at face value, they missed the unexpressed ones and quickly managed to alienate their colleagues. Intending with a good heart to carry out their mandates, they unwittingly violated long-standing norms, and so came across as oppositional and hostile. Predictably, what they got back was hostility. They were eventually frozen out.

MANIPULATIVE NETWORKING VERSUS SINCERE AFFILIATION

Over the past few decades, there has been a lot of talk and much written about networking. It is to our advantage, we are told, to make friends and maintain relationships with those who may be able to help us. Pundits and authors suggest that high-level jobs are almost always filled on the basis of connections.

Having been involved in the hiring of hundreds of high-level people, I regard such advice as largely ridiculous. Sure, contacts can and sometimes do help. But there is a huge industry comprised of search professionals who, more often than not, present a slate of candidates to an organization. Probably fewer than one out of ten external candidates is hired because of connections. I emphasize this because a great many people have become increasing wary of manipulative networking. Personally, I am more likely to help a person who comes straight out and asks for assistance than someone who sidles up to me at a party or through some form of social media.

By all means, be outgoing and attend events that appeal to you. While you're there, be friendly and meet as many people as you *naturally* can. But do nothing that would cause others to view you as trying to befriend them in order to benefit. For collegiality to engender trust, it has to be perceived as genuine, and few of us are good enough actors to fake authenticity.

LOYALTY

I remember a man who was hired as a senior-level sales manager. It wasn't long before he began to put his staff on edge, to voice his critical opinions, and—most relevantly here—to undermine his supervisor in a not-very-ingenious manner.[4] The latter soon found out about this and from then on regarded him as disloyal. When at one point during a restructuring, the supervisor might have gone out of his way to help preserve the man's job, this didn't happen. Loyalty creates trust. Treachery destroys it.

If you want to increase your trust quotient, build friendships grounded in loyalty. Loyalty, like collegiality, tends to be reciprocated. It's a precious commodity that costs nothing but a good heart and a little effort. Among the best ways to build such friendships is to turn your subordinates into stars. A great way to get things done is not to worry about who gets the credit. Unless you're expected to make a particular presentation, let your peers or subordinates make it. Not so often that you look like you're afraid to make one or are evading responsibility, but often enough to engender their loyalty. Make sure they have face time with those above you. Brag about them. Without fostering upward delegation, help them when they need it. Give to them, and all but the worst of them will give back to you, sometimes in abundance.

EIGHT

Assertiveness: Flexibility in Leading and Following

Do you demonstrate the desire to lead and take charge when it's appropriate to do so? Are you inclined to act as a spokesperson, and can you express yourself clearly, cogently, and powerfully? Can you be dominant without becoming dominating or domineering? Are you flexible when it comes to whether to lead or follow, so that you do whichever of the two is appropriate in a given circumstance?

Intellect, stability, and conscientiousness—the first three dimensions of the Big Five—are not by nature interpersonal. They don't need a social context in which to operate. Living alone on an island, you can be smart, stable, and diligent, or dull, neurotic, and lazy.

The final two dimensions of the Big Five are different. They only make sense in a social context. It's difficult to imagine what friendliness or assertiveness would look like if there were no other people around. These dimensions expressly concern how you relate to others, whether you move toward or away/against from them, and one-up or one-down. In the last chapter, we discussed friendliness. In this one, we'll take up the more complex subject of assertiveness.

Assertive people tend to be confident, managerial, and unafraid to use power. They're comfortable giving directions, are generally decisive, and come across as authoritative, persuasive, and influential. Such people like responsibility and have no difficulty giving orders. Those around them tend to view assertive people as natural leaders who some-times act with a fair amount of self-discipline. Highly assertive people push for action. They are determined and forceful, want decisions to be made, and sometimes can be unrealistic about what the organization can accomplish.

Unassertive people are less decisive, directive, and confident. They are not as comfortable using power as their assertive colleagues. Reticent leaders look to others to help orient them to what's going on, and they are comparatively less authoritative, persuasive, and influential. They may also be less systematic and structured. Whereas an assertive person is inclined to talk and lead, an unassertive person is inclined to listen and follow. Those who encounter them are likely to perceive unassertive people as compliant and cooperative. In the face of conflict, the unas-sertive will tend to back away or give in. Such a person may sometimes raise issues that clarify discussions, which can be constructive, but the downside of such behavior is that it can delay closure and decision-making.

I should also point out what has come to be known as the *pursuer-avoider paradigm,* since it often captures what's going on between an as-sertive leader who also micromanages and a subordinate who wants to avoid being micromanaged. The more the pursuer pursues, the more the avoider avoids, and the more the avoider avoids, the more the pursuer pursues. If you find yourself living out the role of avoider with a leader who in response only intensifies the pursuit, it's important to reverse the paradigm. The leader may, for example, keep pressing for additional de-tail. Your natural tendency may be to avoid giving it, on the assumption that doing so will increase the leader's thirst for more. Sometimes the best strategy is to give the leader even larger volumes of information than he or she requests, which can subtly reverse the paradigm's direction, putting you in the role of pursuer.

Two participants in a relationship may be assertive or unassertive, but over time, one of them is likely to become more the leader and the other more the follower. In a healthy relationship, the two will take turns lead-ing, depending on who is more competent in a particular domain. Recall the example of the more verbally capable person writing thank-you notes and the more spatially able one serving as navigator.

We noted in the last chapter how we can use the term *dominance* in place of assertiveness, as long as we understand that dominance can be friendly or hostile. Another way to think about assertiveness, there-fore, is to ask whether you should be dominant or deferent at a particular time. Note that being dominant is not the same as being dominating or domineering, which are hostile forms of dominance (hostile assertion [HA]).

DECISION MAKING

Flexible assertiveness should ideally reflect itself in *how* you approach decisions. As discussed in Chapter 1, some decisions are best made by consensus, in the narrow sense of total agreement. Others should be made through participatory management, whereby you solicit input and then decide. You can also put decisions to a vote. And, there are times when decisions must be made autocratically; if you're in the middle of a crisis, choices must be made quickly, and you may not have time to solicit opinions or count ballots.

Which approach to adopt depends on the challenge or problem before you. Knowing when to use each one is a big part of being an effective leader. It's important that you not make every decision by fiat, acting as a kind of informal dictator, but it is equally important that you not put everything to a vote. Those around you will soon figure out if your primary objective is to avoid responsibility, which is what the voting approach is sometimes intended to do.

READING THE SIGNS

Determining how assertive to be in a particular setting can be tricky. You have to be able to read how much to assert and how much to defer, especially in relation to those above you in the hierarchy. If you don't defer enough, you may pay for it down the line. But if you defer too much or too quickly, you won't be respected, which could cost you a promotion, raise, bonus, or desirable assignment. To further complicate matters, how much to defer depends on the personality of the other person. Some leaders value feistiness, while others regard even tentative disagreement as obstructive, negativistic, and refusing to be a team player.[1]

Remember that flexibility is paramount with this last dimension of the Big Five. You have to know your audience, especially if they outrank you. With certain leaders, it may be functional to imagine you're in a rigidly structured classroom. You're not permitted to raise your hand, lest you interrupt the professor, and you only ask questions when the teacher says it's time to do so. With others, you will fare best if you're energized and participatory, which suggests they expect you to be highly engaged.

The conversation may resemble a fast-moving table tennis match in which you're *supposed* to interrupt. The faster the game, the better.

There is a further complication. Some who outrank you may want you to behave one way with them in private, perhaps assertively, and another way in public, for example when the two of you are in a meeting. Among the more refined art forms of organizational life is learning how to pick up these sorts of subtleties, and your ultimate success may hinge on how well you do this.

It is nearly always to your advantage to be friendly, as long as you don't end up reinforcing abusive behavior. People tend to match each other on warmth, so if you're friendly, the other person is also likely to be friendly. The more alliances you create, the more you can usually get done, so the higher you are on the collegiality scale, the better. This is also true for the first three dimensions of the Big Five. It's better to be more, rather than less, intelligent, stable, and motivated. This is not the case, however, with assertion, where flexibility is paramount.

If someone in a meeting is going down a path you know to be wrong, you must decide whether it's worth the price you could potentially pay for pointing this out—an assertive act. You might end up causing embarrassment, perhaps by making the other person appear incompetent. We discussed in Chapter 5 the wisdom of paying no unnecessary social prices. Sometimes, however, paying the price may be necessary. You may have to decide, on the fly, whether the issue is important enough to the organization for you to risk injuring or alienating a colleague or—even higher stakes—a supervisor.

For several years, one senior executive I know had to make this kind of decision almost daily in relation to someone senior to him. Although the latter was an intelligent enough person, he had little in-depth knowledge of the business, and his judgment was by no means flawless. The two would sometimes be in a meeting with five or six other executives, and the senior of the two would sometimes give out time-consuming assignments that made little sense. His actions call to mind the words of Peter F. Drucker: "So much of what we call management consists in making it difficult for people to work."

What would you do? If you try to stop him, there's a good chance things will turn awkward. You could end up humiliating the leader, or prompt him to conclude you're insubordinate. If you don't try to stop him, however, you may have to spend the rest of the day, if not the week, pulling back counterproductive assignments. And that's only after you've done the hard work of persuading him of their lack of merit. You'll also have to find a way, without lying, to do this in a manner that does not cause others to lose respect for him. It's not easy getting the toothpaste back into the tube.

A MYTHICAL WALL

Some of my professional colleagues like to draw a distinction between assertion and aggression. While such a distinction may work in theory, it tends to break down in practice. If you become assertive enough, your behavior will turn aggressive; because there's no concrete wall between the two, assertion can almost imperceptibly merge into aggression.

Imagine, for example, that your formal wear is in the cleaners, and you need to wear it this evening for an important event. The shop is scheduled to close at 6:00 P.M., which is what the painted lettering on the window reads. You get there at 5:50, only to find the door locked and a *Closed* sign posted. But you notice that the shopkeeper is walking around inside, so you knock. "We're closed," he shouts through the door. You respond, "I need my clothes. You don't close until six." To which he replies with irritation, "Come back tomorrow." What psychologists call *negative escalation* is now underway.

What may *not* break down are your personal limits, how far you're willing to travel on the road from assertion to aggression. And, you might well have different limits depending on context. I would certainly have a different threshold for aggression if I were walking at night with my wife down a dimly lit street in an unfamiliar city than I would at a social event or family gathering.

Unless you are in the military or a member of a police force, you are unlikely to face physical challenges, but you may encounter someone who's becoming distinctly aggressive—not to the point of making physical threats, but to the level of a spirited debate morphing into a heated argument. While there's no foolproof formula for knowing what to do in every circumstance, you can't un-ring the bell. Once you say or do it, you may never be able to restore the relationship to its former glory. So, use caution. Be wise.

STRIVING FOR CLOSURE

The art of good leadership involves ensuring you've communicated your expectations clearly. But it also involves making sure you know what's expected by those above you. I've been astonished by the distorting effects of wishful thinking on memory. People will sometimes remember events as they wish, not as they actually happened. Never agree to do anything unless you fully understand what is expected. You and the person making the request or demand *must* reach a meeting of the minds.

Ask questions about anything you don't understand, and say back to the other person what you've just heard, to avoid going down the wrong track. The same words can mean very different things to different people. Words can be vague, ambiguous, and elusive, so make sure you nail down exactly what the other person wants. Be assertive about this, even if the one to whom you owe the deliverable makes you feel stupid. You're only stupid if you fail to verify expectations.

CULTURAL FIT

Every organization has a culture and often a series of subcultures that more or less prescribe how assertive you are expected to be. If you work as a military officer, you're supposed to command. To what extent depends, of course, on which branch of the armed forces you're in, and beyond this, in what specialty. SEALS are part of the United States Navy, but the expectations of their subculture more closely resemble those of Army Rangers than naval surface warfare officers. The same is true for Marines, who are a Department of the Navy. If, by contrast, you work for a charitable organization whose well-being depends on donations, the expectations around assertive behavior are likely to be more infused with tact and graciousness.

In an organization that highly values assertion, you will be more persuasive if you are forceful rather than timid. Your opportunities for increased responsibility will also be greater, and you will find yourself more at home. The opposite will be true if you're in an organization whose culture shies away from conflict and confrontation. Such an organization is not necessarily the place for someone who has a high need to speak up, decide how things get done, or control outcomes, and who may not worry a great deal about the harmony index.

When an organization prizes assertiveness, it will emphasize accountability and decisiveness. But it may also foster keen competition between and among colleagues. This amounts to zero-sum game thinking, my win is your loss, and your win is my loss. Such thinking may, in fact, reflect reality. Strict hierarchical obedience may emerge, and most of the power in the organization will reside in the hands of a few. When, to the contrary, an organization regards assertive behavior as bad form and therefore to be avoided, power will be more widely distributed. There will be more negotiation but less efficiency, as well as less single-point accountability. Emphasis on the feel-good quotient will be high, and as a result, leaders will be reluctant to challenge one another. In such an organization, preserving self-esteem, especially of high-ranking leaders, may sometimes be even more important than making good decisions.

If your natural style matches the culture in which you find yourself, the members of that culture will be more inclined to trust you, which implies they will be more likely to look to you for leadership. They will be comfortable. Even if your natural style does not match the culture, having the capacity to adapt to its norms, and therefore to what the organization subtly requires, will enable you to fit in. Such adapting may not always be easy, but you will probably be okay as long as you stay motivated to adapt. Sometimes, however, the norms of the culture are so different from what you're comfortable with that you will only survive in it with chronic tension. If this is the case, it may be time to look for another job.

INFLEXIBLE DEFERENCE

Some people are routinely deferential, to the point of being reflexively compliant if not submissive. They'll work fourteen hours a day rather than insist that their subordinates put in even one extra hour. I once knew a leader who had to resign from his company because he couldn't bring himself to demand results. He wouldn't *insist,* so he'd end up working late into the night. His subordinates were managing him more than the reverse. Work, as we have noted, involves doing a lot of things that we might not otherwise choose to do, and part of being an effective leader is getting others to do what you need them to.

Leaders who are excessively deferential give others the impression that they are not firm or decisive. They may also be criticized for inaction and lack of clear direction. Such impressions and critiques may be unjust and unwise. Sometimes, no doubt, they are. Regardless, they are likely to be applied to any leader in a hierarchical organizational who has a low need for control. People in organizations have to be led, and they tend to be drawn toward those who, without ambivalence, want to lead them.

INFLEXIBLE DOMINANCE

Some people are rigidly dominant. They insist on taking charge, even when it would be better to let someone else lead. Executives and managers like this may *say* they value healthy conflict or creative dissent, but that's only if you agree with them, if you "recognize right answer when told." Wise leaders understand there's a time to take charge, and a time to let someone else take charge, even if that person reports to them. Theodore Roosevelt put it this way: "The best executive is the one who has sense enough to pick good men to do what he wants done, and self-restraint enough to keep from meddling with them while they do it."

Few leaders make it to the top tier of an organization without a strong need to assert. This is why the top two executives in organizations often engage in a silent war of mutual disrespect. If and when their tensions escalate to an outright war, one of them—typically the more junior of the two—will often leave. Thus, sometimes even a high-ranking executive will become unhinged and eventually undone by an inability to flex.

Leaders who are rigidly dominant tend to be task-focused. They want to get the job done without fanfare and meet deadlines without slippage. As a breed, they value structure, handing out assignments, refusing to reverse decisions they've made, and establishing challenging objectives. If they take all of this too far, however, they can come across as overbearing, insensitive, and ruthless—willing to sacrifice others to get to the goal, whatever that goal happens to be. The rest of the world becomes cannon fodder.

I have consulted for a few companies in which the CEO and chief operating officer (COO) got along marvelously. In each instance, one of several conditions seemed to obtain. Either the COO respected the CEO and carried no ill will over *not* being in the top spot. Or, there was a division of labor between the two that made enormous practical sense; the CEO was gifted as an external representative of the enterprise, while the COO was capable of running its real-time operations. When the COO respects and is loyal to the CEO, the COO may be younger and hope, eventually, to be appointed CEO. Or, the COO may be closer to retirement and does not aspire to win the top job.

Sometimes they get along well simply because of the exemplary character of the COO. It would never occur to the number two to be anything other than loyal to, and well aligned with, the CEO. If you spoke to either of them, therefore, you might as well be speaking to the other—you're going to get the same response.

DELEGATION VERSUS ABDICATION

If you empower people rather than micromanaging them, they will often surprise you by what they will accomplish. Entrusting them with responsibility can go a long way toward building their self-esteem, as well as further enrolling and enfranchising them in your vision, mission, goals, programs, projects, and strategies. One by-product of empowering subordinates is that you won't have to work as hard. Keep in mind, however, the maxim popularized by former President Ronald Reagan: *trust but verify.* Delegation does not mean abdication.

Early in my career, I failed to verify something, with near-disastrous consequences. My consulting practice was growing rapidly, work was coming at me from all sides, and I was scrambling to keep up. The eight-year-old daughter of another consultant, when he told her he was having trouble keeping up with his work, remarked, "Daddy, maybe you need to be in a slower group." That's about how I felt.

It was September and a company asked me to collect anonymous feedback—numerical ratings and verbal comments—on ninety director-level leaders. The directors were to receive the results at a conference scheduled for October.

I had a technologically savvy associate working for me at the time, and it was his job to ensure that, for each director, the verbal comments were properly sorted and entered into a database. He also had responsibility for exporting the numerical ratings into a spreadsheet program so they could be automatically averaged. Finally, to produce the confidential individualized reports, he was to export the verbal comments and averaged ratings from the database and spreadsheet program into documents generated using a word processor. He'd tested all of the steps again and again. The process was working wonderfully.

About a week before the conference, I asked him to make a minor change in how the ratings were displayed in the reports. I *assumed*—that nasty word!—he would check to make sure the three programs (database, spreadsheet, word processor) continued to function as intended. But he neglected to do this and I neglected to check. I remember feeling very good as I stood up on the first day of the conference to tell the directors that each of them would be assigned to one of ten breakout rooms, where they would be given their results.

Less than ten minutes after the main room cleared, one of the directors walked toward me and whispered, "All the numbers are the same." To which I replied, "I don't need this right now, Eric. This is no time for jokes." Then, the human resources executive who had organized the conference stormed up. "Where's the quality control?"

Every report had the ratings that belonged to the man whose name appeared first in an alphabetized list, which is what everyone immediately assumed. Fortunately, his ratings were excellent. I had not yet deleted the data, so I was able to assure the directors at dinner that corrected reports would be in their hands within a few days.

People in that company were more understanding than I could have wished, for which I am still grateful, and I continue to consult for them. This story poignantly illustrates how imprudent delegation and follow-up can have profound consequences.

HOW TO ASSERT WITHOUT ALIENATING

Over twenty years ago, an executive gave me the following advice: "When you want to accomplish something, especially if it's unpopular and you're likely to encounter resistance, apply *gentle unrelenting pressure.*" Rather than pushing so hard that you run into a barricade or have to endure countless rounds of foot-dragging, just keep at it in a low-keyed way. Water, dripping on a rock, eventually prevails. It isn't the gentle force of any single drop but their long-term cumulative impact.

As a consultant, I have no place in the organization chart and therefore no position power. I can't make things happen by issuing directives. So, I often have to *time-sell* my ideas. Sometimes, I have to keep at it for years, but sooner or later my more worthy recommendations are implemented, if for no other reason than that I rarely give up. Patience and persistence bring results, but only if you don't alienate those you want to influence.

Another approach to asserting without alienating is to use *negative timing*—you don't say *yes* or *no;* you defer the decision. Imagine that you chair the board of directors for a nonprofit. Half of the directors strongly desire to change its name and the other half vehemently oppose such a change. You are the deciding vote. It might be wise to table the question, at least temporarily, rather than to risk immediately alienating 50 percent of the board by aligning with one side or the other.

DEALING WITH PROBLEM CHILDREN

There may be occasions when you have several underperforming subordinates and conclude they all either have to be put on probation or their employment terminated. If so, it's important to approach this challenge methodically. Deal with them one at a time, lest they bond together, complain about you to human resources, and make *you* look like the problem child.

If this happens, they'll claim you're unfair, your demands are unreasonable, you're destroying morale, and so forth. And, they'll get considerable sympathy from long-term friends in the organization who may remain unaware of the deficient performance. Troublesome subordinates may informally unionize against you, with support from outside your organization, and foment a revolt.

It's usually wise to take care of your biggest personnel problem first. Move on to the next only after you've achieved a satisfactory resolution, whether this is getting the person back on track through coaching, putting him or her on probation, or resorting to the ultimate weapon of termination.

TAKING INVENTORY

Here are some questions for self-reflection. Take your time to work through them thoughtfully. And, be sure to answer truthfully. My second-favorite Chinese proverb[2] applies in part to being honest with ourselves: *Gain power by accepting reality.*

- How much do you put yourself forward in meetings?
- To what extent do you prefer to take charge?
- How much do you hold back?
- To what degree do you wait for others to lead?
- Do you pay enough attention to rank and how sensitive each person around you may be to it—how hierarchical (authoritarian) versus egalitarian (democratic)?
- Do you, on the contrary, pay too much attention to it?
- Do you advance your ideas and opinions at the expense of others?
- To what extent do you rely on those above you to tell you what to do?
- How much do you depend on peers to give you work direction?
- Do you express resistance to ideas simply to establish your independence?
- To what extent do you allow others to assert themselves?
- How willing are you to ask for help when you need it?
- Can you learn to live more comfortably with ambiguity?
- Do you include everyone who should attend your meetings?
- Do you make sure you understand all instructions and directives before you begin?
- Are you willing to push back on assignments that are beyond you?
- Do you more often ask permission or forgiveness?

All of these questions relate, directly or indirectly, to assertiveness.

CAN IT BE DONE?

Knowing when to assert yourself and your ideas, and when to go along with the ideas and wishes of others, requires intuitive savvy. You can't be a clod and have good outcomes. Yet, even if you know when to act assertively, you may still have to muster up the courage to do so.

When you assert, you are issuing an overture for others to defer. There's always the risk that they'll refuse, perhaps by openly opposing you. We all differ in our levels of risk tolerance. Some jump out of airplanes while others refuse even to board them. Can a person learn to be more or less assertive?

I had to learn to command when I became a cadet officer in a military academy, especially since the academy I attended was a highly disciplined and buttoned-down place, run almost entirely by cadets who were expected to be unambiguously forceful. At first, telling others what to do—issuing commands and barking orders—felt strange and awkward. It was not something that came naturally. It comes naturally to very few, if any, of us. Even drill sergeants have to acquire what's been labeled the *mask of command.*[3] Most people, I believe, can acquire the necessary mask. They just have to want to.

When you're installed in a position of leadership, a role and a set of responsibilities come along with it. One implication of this is that, as noted earlier, there is no such thing as off-duty time, at least not when you're with people from the same organization. You're always *in role,* whether or not you realize it. You can ignore or forget this only at your peril. Whether it's a company party around the holidays or an off-site conference at a resort, your role includes unstated but important behavioral prescriptions. Many of the prescriptions have to do with self-control and assertiveness.

Role prescriptions and corresponding expectations often make leadership a solitary business. "It's lonely at the top" is more than a cliché; it's a pithy description of organizational life. Those with whom you spend a third to half of your waking hours will always, of necessity, remain part of your audience, an audience to whom you owe the duty to meet these role expectations. Shakespeare knew what he was writing about when, in a line from *As You Like It,* he suggested, "All the world's a stage." Surely, an organization is.

Recall our discussion in Chapter 5 about the need to avoid dual-role relationships. In that chapter, we discussed why it's unwise to become a long-term confidant and counselor to subordinates. But, you can't afford to become emotionally dependent on them either. This makes close friendships inside organizations difficult. The peer who listens patiently to the problems you're having today may turn out to be the same person who, in a year or two, may become an underperforming subordinate you'll have to put on a performance improvement plan (PIP).

If you fulfill your duty to stay in role, others will tend to trust you. And, if you default on it, they will not. If they don't trust you, they will never embrace you as their leader.

Before moving on to Part II in Chapter 10, where we will focus on the key facets of interpersonal effectiveness, here's a quick review of the dimensions of the Big Five:

- *Intellect:* The ability to get your mind around concepts, think logically, develop sound implementation plans, and grasp the big picture; analytic and intuitive reasoning.
- *Stability:* Basic maturity, predictability, and the absence of psychological interference; good signal-to-noise ratio.
- *Conscientiousness:* Being a closer, but even before that, being an opener—showing proactivity; doing whatever it takes to get things done and achieve results.
- *Friendliness:* Establishing and maintaining collaborative and nonpredatory relationships; being loyal and trustworthy; not engaging in manipulative behavior.
- *Assertiveness:* Wanting to take charge; allowing others to take charge when appropriate; showing flexibility when it comes to control.

The power of viewing them in combination will become apparent in the next chapter.

NINE

Sample Profiles

As we saw in Chapter 3, if we use only three levels of evaluation—high, medium, low—on each dimension of the Big Five, we end up with a surprisingly large number of possible profiles: 243. And, if we use five levels—high, medium high, medium, medium low, and low—we get a whopping 3,125 profiles.

Although, in order to emphasize positive motivation, I titled Chapter 6 "Conscientiousness," in the profiles depicted here I've used the more general term *motivation*. This is to allow the diagrams to conform more closely to the equation $P = A \times M$ (Performance = Ability × Motivation) and also to demonstrate that in some of the profiles motivation is neither positive nor constructive.

Using only three levels, it is possible to construct the profile of someone we might think of as having an *ideal leadership pattern* (Figure 9.1). This is the person who has it all. I have met a few such individuals; although rare, they do exist.

Recall how one characteristic of a good leader is the ability to regulate assertiveness so that it's appropriate to the context. Assertiveness is therefore depicted as an arrow, rather than a bar, to illustrate the need for flexibility. In addition to using this profile to think about your leadership qualities, you can also use it as a template for evaluating those you are considering for employment or promotion.

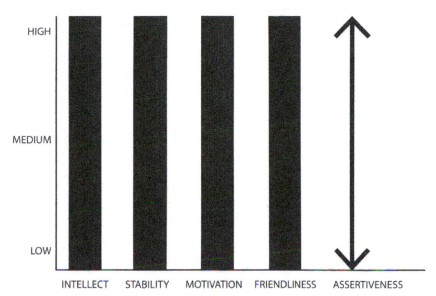

Figure 9.1   Ideal Leadership Pattern

Below are nine more profiles that demonstrate the power of the Big Five to help you identify and understand some common patterns of designated leaders. Not all the labels are flattering. Note that, in each example, I have depicted *only the dimensions that define the basic pattern.* Ignore the dimensions that do not have a bar above them. Treat the missing bars as irrelevant or secondary to the pattern depicted.

Let's return once more to $P = A \times M$. Although much more goes into high performance as a leader, these two dimensions are directly relevant to every person in every job, from the cafeteria worker to the CEO. You can think of them as threshold attributes; they are necessary but not sufficient. The levels of ability and motivation required vary from position to position, but not their fundamental relevance. A person with neither talent nor drive might be thought of as a *flatliner,* depicted in Figure 9.2.

Some people do very well in organizations because they are stable and motivated. They might not be rocket scientists, but they are smart enough to do good work. Here is what such a person's profile might look like. I call this one the *reliable overachiever* (Figure 9.3) to highlight how there is often a trade-off between ability and motivation. Highly capable people don't have to work as hard as the less capable, but those with the *reliable overachiever* profile can still contribute significantly.

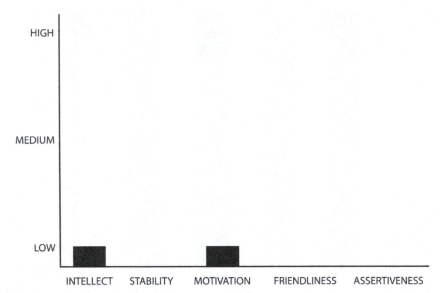

Figure 9.2   Flatliner

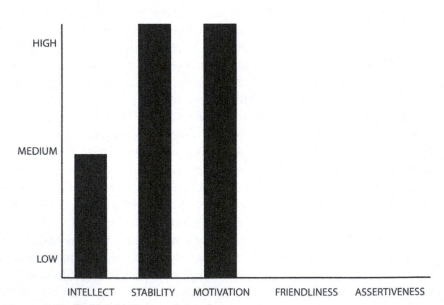

Figure 9.3   Reliable Overachiever

A commonly observed pattern is the *productive introverted analyst*, illustrated in Figure 9.4. This is the person who contributes most when not managing others. Such an individual is not a "people person" and usually prefers to work alone. Nor does such a person show much interest in providing work direction to others, or following up to make sure they are doing what they're supposed to be doing. This is the profile for many lab scientists who sometimes become so absorbed in intellectual activity that they forget to eat. Ability is high and so is motivation, while friendliness and assertiveness are low.

Next is the profile of someone who has considerable ability but remains without sufficient motivation to excel in a high-level position. I call this one the *nonexecutive solid performer.* This pattern is portrayed in Figure 9.5.

Figures 9.6–9.8 depict disruptive employees. The first is the *loose cannon*, shown in Figure 9.6. Another colloquial term for such a person is an *unguided missile.* It fits those who are unstable but have a high level of motivation, and in this case it is not particularly good. They therefore have the motivation to infect others with their instability, and by implication to inflict pain on both people and organizations.

What happens if we add high intelligence to this profile? We end up with what I think of as the *dangerous loose cannon* (Figure 9.7). This is someone who has the intelligence to graduate from problem child to organizational

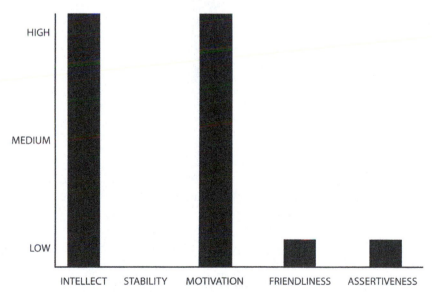

Figure 9.4   Productive Introverted Analyst

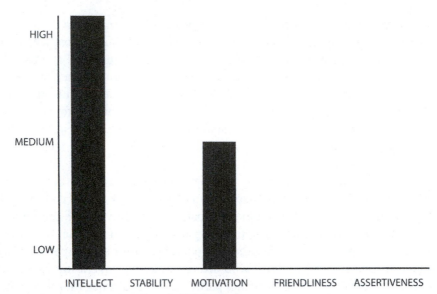

Figure 9.5   Non-executive Solid Performer

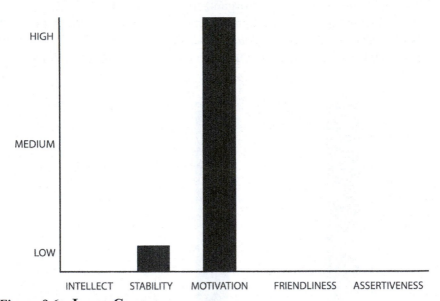

Figure 9.6   Loose Cannon

menace. People with this profile are clever enough to manipulate those around them and, sometimes, to enroll them in counterproductive causes.

Now, let's add high dominance to the mix, as depicted in Figure 9.8. The result is someone who is unstable, motivated, and smart, but in addition inclined to take control and dominate others. Adolf Hitler exemplified this

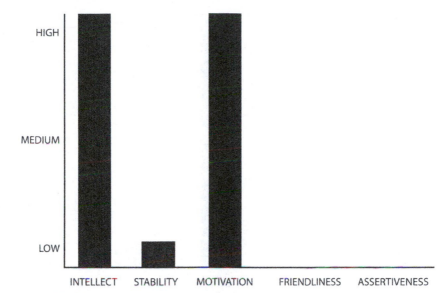

Figure 9.7   Dangerous Loose Cannon

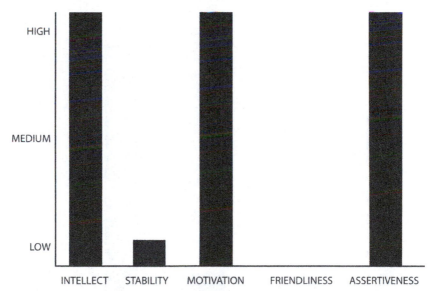

Figure 9.8   Very Dangerous Loose Cannon

profile. So do many other dictators. It is the profile of the *very dangerous loose cannon.*

Next, we come to the profile of the *autocrat,* shown in Figure 9.9. This is someone who is high on the *task* dimension of management but low on the *relationship* one. He or she does not much care about being friendly

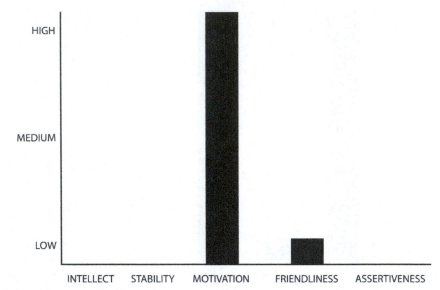

Figure 9.9   Autocrat

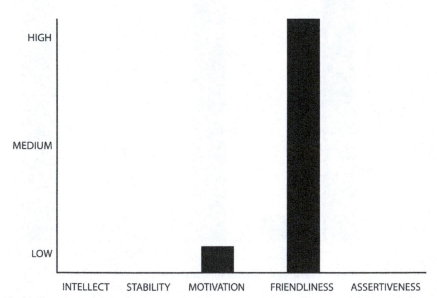

Figure 9.10   Country Club Manager

and liked. All that matters is getting the work done, no matter whom it hurts or inconveniences.

Finally, we come to what has sometimes been called the *country club manager* (Figure 9.10), not to be confused with the manager of an actual country club, who may work exceedingly hard. This person is the opposite of the autocrat, and therefore high on collegiality but low on initiative. The harmony quotient is important; getting the work done is not. All country club managers are underachievers, but not all underachievers are social enough to be country club managers. Many of these managers do reasonably well because those who work for them are loyal and therefore motivated to make sure things get done. They cover for their boss.

We have examined only ten—roughly 4 percent—of the 243 possible profiles. The Big Five is an exceedingly powerful tool, not because it can generate over 200 profiles—any collection of five attributes rated as high, medium, or low could do that—but, rather, because the profiles it yields are based on the dimensions that *most predict performance*. Not perfectly of course, but better than anything else in the marketplace.

Think carefully about what your profile is. It might be useful to ask for feedback from peers, listen carefully to what they tell you, and try to infer which profile they would construct for you. This should give you a good start on homing in on your primary assets and principal developmental need.

PART II

Leadership and Interpersonal Savvy

FACETS OF INTERPERSONAL BEHAVIOR

Insight: Knowing yourself well enough to understand how your moods, feelings, thoughts, and attitudes affect your behavior; and quickly grasping the impact you have on others.

Restraint: Showing the ability to control your impulses, especially hostile ones when irritated or provoked; effectively monitoring and modulating what you say and do.

Nobility: Genuinely caring about the welfare of the organization; striking a balance between taking care of yourself and taking care of others; working for a higher cause than compensation and benefits.

Compassion: Being able quickly and accurately to detect and identify with the feelings of others; demonstrating that you comprehend what they're going through and that you care.

Persuasiveness: Building on the four assets explained above, having the ability to influence others so they support you and your objectives and do what they might not otherwise choose to do; obtaining their buy-in.

TEN

Introduction to Interpersonal Effectiveness

Industrial psychologists have traditionally argued that intelligence is the best predictor of performance. But it appears—no surprise—that, for effectiveness as a leader, certain *kinds* of intelligence are more important than others. These sometimes get lumped under the catchy term *emotional intelligence,*[1] but it may be stretching the word intelligence too far to apply it to all of them. I prefer to think of the five facets of personality we are about to take up as attributes that contribute to interpersonal effectiveness (IE). They are foundational to good leadership.

A quote attributed to John Quincy Adams suggests, "If your actions inspire others to dream more, learn more, do more and become more, you are a leader." Management has largely to do with getting work done *through* other people, which highlights the importance of interpersonal skill. People high on IE are typically persuasive. They have a natural ability to negotiate and are therefore able to find common ground with others and come up with win–win as opposed to win–lose solutions. Skilled at leading change, they have a kind of inner sense, a feel for when to use power and when to rely on social influence. I have watched an executive stand up in front of hundreds of employees he was unavoidably about to lay off, while those employees remained civil, respectful, and loyal. I have also watched executives end up with mutinies as a result of making trivial changes.

The capacities that create the foundation for IE are not as straightforward as the dimensions of the Big Five, the source traits from which they largely derive. As highlighted in Part I, the dimensions of the Big Five are for all practical purposes uncorrelated. Knowing where someone stands on any one of the five tells you nothing about where he or she stands on any of the other four. Facets of IE, however, *are* correlated. If you're high on insight, for example, there is a greater than average chance you'll also be high on empathy. Still, the five facets of IE are sufficiently distinct to merit thinking about and discussing them separately. As suggested by the brief descriptions on the preceding page, the first four facets of IE flow into, foster, and enhance persuasiveness; of the five, this is the one most clearly relevant to leadership.

Leadership, as we have seen, is the ability to enroll and enfranchise others into your vision, mission, goals, programs, projects, strategies, and tactics. Antoine de Saint-Exupéry, author of *The Little Prince,* put it this way: "If you want to build a ship, don't drum up people together to collect wood and don't assign them tasks and work, but rather teach them to long for the endless immensity of the sea." Others will only follow you from the heart if you persuade them to do so—if you inspire them. Otherwise, they'll just go through the motions. They may superficially conform, but they will not internalize what you want them to. And, once again, you will not be able to persuade them if they do not trust you, if you don't connect with them. To the extent they perceive you as interpersonally attuned, they will be disposed to trust. If they trust, they will be inclined to follow.

A good test of your leadership would be to charge up a hill against enemy fire, and then turn around to see if your platoon's still there. Another test would be to find out what your subordinates do when you're not watching. If the measure of your manners is what you do when no one's looking, the measure of your leadership is what subordinates do when you're not looking—which will be determined to a considerable extent by how well you've managed to connect with them. As is true of the Big Five, some facets of IE are more relevant to how they see your competence, and other facets to how they see your character, but all of them are important.

I want briefly to consider how the dimensions of the Big Five relate to the five facets of IE, and how they function as root causes. We want to ask how the *source traits* of the five-factor model contribute to the *derivative traits* of IE.

A useful way to think about this relationship draws on ideas from genetics. Biologists speak of a person's *genotype* versus *phenotype. Genotype* is the array of genes someone is born with. It's that person's genetic constitution or, as biologists call it, *genetic complement.* These genes are contained in an individual's forty-six pair of chromosomes, each made up of DNA. Except for cells involved in sexual reproduction, which contain only twenty-three chromosomes, the same forty-six are housed in the nucleus of every cell in a person's body. The cells in the cornea of your eye, for example, have the exact same genes as those in your foot. It's just that, as we develop, different genes in different parts of the body get expressed or suppressed at different rates, so we grow eyes and feet where they should be. Apart from mutations, caused for example by prolonged exposure to ultraviolet light, genes are not expected to change; they are hardwired into the chromosomes.[2]

Phenotype, by contrast, refers to a person's observable characteristics. It is how a genotype gets *expressed,* and so, unlike genes, it may be, but is not in all cases, influenced by a person's environment or developmental experience.

It's not always clear how much a given characteristic is determined by genetics and how much by environment or experience—how much by *nature* and how much by *nurture.* If you were well nourished as a child you are probably taller than you otherwise would have been, but how large a role nutrition plays in determining the height of any one individual is not obvious. The same is true for intelligence. The biological children of highly intelligent parents tend, on average, to be more intelligent than the offspring of less gifted parents. But highly intelligent parents also tend to value education and therefore to cultivate cognitive development. Again, for any given person growing up, it is unclear how much enhanced cultivation contributes to measured intelligence.

This is the analogy we want to construct: A:B :: C:D. A (Big Five) is to B (interpersonal effectiveness) *as* C (genotype) is to D (phenotype). The Big Five are a kind of psychological genotype, while the components of IE are the phenotype.

Like all analogies, this one breaks down if you push it too far; the Big Five, for example, is *not* a set of physical genes that, apart from mutations, are believed by most biologists not to change; the dimensions of the Big Five are more malleable. Every dimension of the Big Five, including intellect, is in reality the reflection of a collection of many genes *interacting* with environment and experience: nature *plus* nurture. Still, it is useful to think of these dimensions as source traits that, in some combination, underlie a great deal of what people actually do.[3]

Another metaphor that can help us understand the relationship between the Big Five and IE is to think of the dimensions of the Big Five as elements in a small periodic table. The derivative traits making up IE are compounds that can be made from these elements. Sodium and chlorine, when appropriately combined, make sodium chloride, common table salt. But chlorine can also be combined with potassium to yield potassium chloride, a salt substitute. Similarly, sodium can be combined with other elements, for example carbon, hydrogen, and oxygen to make sodium bicarbonate (baking soda).

A third way to make sense of the relationship between the Big Five and IE is to imagine each of the facets of IE as a cake. Most cakes are made from flour, sweetener, eggs, milk or water, fat such as butter or shortening, flavoring, and baking power. It is by no means obvious from the finished cake how much of each ingredient it contains.

It is exceedingly difficult to specify how a complex set of behaviors reflects *both* the source traits of the Big Five and the derivative traits of IE. Nonetheless, in trying to understand leadership, it is important to focus on these ten traits, rather than countless others, real or imagined, that would explain and predict little or nothing.

We could, for example, simply say that a person's effectiveness as a leader depends on leadership ability—as if this were a single and easy-to-measure trait. It most certainly is not, which is why nowhere in this book do I refer to leadership as a single trait or ability. It is not, for example, simply assertiveness (see the sample profiles in Chapter 9). Worse, to try to explain leadership in terms of leadership *ability* is a tautology—the explanation goes around in circles:

"Why is Kate such an effective leader?"

"Because she has lots of leadership ability."

"How do we know she has such leadership ability?"

"Because she's an effective leader."

As an example of looking in the wrong place, imagine an inebriated fellow walking home from a party at midnight. He begins looking for his missing watch under a streetlamp. A kind-hearted policeman offers to help, and inquires about exactly where he lost it. To this, the man replies, "Down the street." Surprised, the policeman asks, "Then why are you looking for it here?" "Because," slurs the man, "there's more light here."

Trying to figure out exactly how the Big Five and the facets of IE account for complex behavior is like looking for the watch down the street in the dark. It's easier to search under the streetlight, but that's not where we'll find what we're looking for. We need to search where we're most likely to succeed, not where it's convenient. As suggested above, it doesn't get us very far to try to explain leadership in a simplistic or circular way, or to resort to an arbitrary set of capacities whose major virtue is face validity.[4]

AN EXAMPLE

Let's examine the attributes that appear to be needed in those who are able to negotiate a satisfactory labor agreement. I picked this outcome because achieving it demands a lot of interrelated behaviors. We'll look first at the Big Five, then at two of the five facets of interpersonal effectiveness, and finally at how the latter may relate to the former.

To succeed at labor negotiations, a person has to have a keen mind (intellect) since such negotiations are intricate and complicated, with many fast-moving parts. He or she also has to be mature because negotiations can continue long into the night, from Monday to Friday and sometimes on weekends. Sticking with them without losing patience requires steadiness and emotional resilience (stability). Then, there's determination. For negotiations to succeed, you have to want them to work (conscientiousness). And, being amiable might help (friendliness), since there's no point in angering those sitting across from you at the bargaining table—no reason to provoke them into becoming obstructive or retaliatory. Finally, a certain amount of ascendance or dominance may be needed (assertiveness). You're unlikely to be good at negotiating if you're timid. But, you can't be too assertive either, lest negotiations degenerate into a power struggle.

With this kind of armchair analysis we can see the necessity of the Big Five, but we don't know how much of each dimension is needed. Nor do we know, for any one of the five dimensions, the specifics. We don't know, for example, how high intellect has to be, or whether analytic reasoning or conceptual thinking is more important. Moving on to the other four dimensions, how much stability is required? And, where exactly does a labor negotiator have to fall on measures of conscientiousness, friendliness, or assertiveness? Let's turn, now, to a couple of facets of IE involved in labor negotiations. What role do *they* play, and how do they relate to the Big Five?

Having the wherewithal to remain calm under pressure and, thus, not be provoked into saying or doing something imprudent (restraint) is important. So is the talent to bring others around to your point of view, and beyond that, to get them to commit on the basis of such a shift without worrying about losing face (persuasiveness). The other three facets—insight, nobility, and sensitivity—no doubt also play a role, but in the interest of brevity we'll limit our discussion to self-restraint, with passing mention of persuasiveness.

Restraint, as we'll see, is the ability to control the expression of impulses, to refrain from physical or verbal acting out. Like the other facets of IE, this one is developed and refined as we grow up and develop. Relating it as best we can to the Big Five, it is determined largely by a person's stability, since stability makes self-control easier: unstable people find it harder to hold back, to harness their impulses. But restraint also relates to intellect, conscientiousness, and friendliness. Intellect may be important, since a person who demonstrates restraint usually has the capacity to recognize that lack of restraint is counterproductive, and also to anticipate the adverse consequences of lashing out. Conscientiousness can also facilitate impulse control. The negotiator has to have the desire to act in the way most likely to achieve a positive result. And, people high on friendliness may hesitate to act out their feelings because they prefer not to alienate or offend others. But, again, how much of each—stability, intellect, conscientiousness, friendliness—is needed? What's the formula? And, how much does the formula vary from situation to situation?

I won't attempt this kind of root-cause analysis for persuasiveness, except to note that it probably reflects some combination of friendliness, intellect, and stability, with assertiveness thrown in. Again, the formula remains a mystery.[5]

CAN YOU INCREASE INTERPERSONAL EFFECTIVENESS?

Something of an industry has emerged in the form of seminars and workshops offering to increase emotional intelligence. At least a few of them seem to overpromise results. As with the Big Five, changing IE takes concentrated and prolonged effort. Significantly increasing it is not likely to be achieved quickly.

But, with the right strategies and reasonable diligence, you can (1) become more psychologically and socially insightful, (2) learn to regulate your impulses better, (3) decrease off-putting self-centeredness, (4) develop more interpersonal sensitivity, and (5) increase how persuasive you are. These, of course, refer to the five facets of IE. It just takes effort and the willingness to ask for feedback—regularly, persistently, sincerely, openly, and nondefensively. We will discuss exactly how best to do this in the next chapter.

The chapters that follow contain concrete strategies for increasing IE. But, for these strategies to succeed, you have to use them, to make them part of your ongoing life as a leader. Begin by keeping a journal of what works and what doesn't. Your perceptions will not always perfectly correspond to what actually happened, but writing them down will help you start to think systematically about interpersonal encounters.

This journal should contain entries of every significant interaction you have. What was the nature of the exchange? What was your objective? How did you go about trying to reach it? Did that work? If so, why? And, if it didn't work, why do you think that was? Don't put your journal on your organization's server, or leave it in your desk. This is a private document intended for self-development, not something to leave lying around for others to peruse.

It's also a good idea to keep a log of how you spend your time. Do this for a few weeks. Such a time-log can prove enlightening, painfully perhaps but always productively. It may give you clues about why certain behaviors are not working. If, for example, you're not as persuasive as you'd like to be, it may be because you're spending too little time with the people you'd most like to persuade.

BE PATIENT

If, on average, over the course of a long career in major league baseball, a player gets a hit one out of three times, it's a ticket to the Hall of Fame. You don't have to bat 1,000—.333 (33.3%) will do. No one plays a perfect game. Be patient with your progress. If you genuinely care about your effectiveness as a leader, you will almost certainly increase it.

ELEVEN

Insight: Knowing Yourself and Your Impact

Are you self-aware, able to detect when your emotions are spilling over and intruding into your work? How about when your personal biases are getting in the way of acting wisely or—equally importantly for a leader—fairly? Do you sense how you are coming across to an audience? Can you accurately read how what you say or do is received, or are you relatively oblivious to your impact? To what extent are you aware of how others view you—can you see yourself through their eyes?

You have probably encountered at least a few people who are glaringly lacking in self-awareness. They manage to stumble through life without realizing how their moods affect their actions, how their biases influence their judgments, or how their past experiences condition their attitudes. Such people are blind to how their emotions, strengths, weaknesses, needs, or ambitions influence what they think, say, and do.

People without insight into themselves sometimes also lack the social radar needed to detect how they come across. Oblivious to their impact, they routinely fail to pick up on the cues that would tell them when others are bored, irritated, tuned out, frustrated, or unresponsive. The eyes of everyone in the room could glaze over and they wouldn't notice. Like a captain on the high seas with no idea of where the ship is, it is almost impossible for them to switch to a more productive course—to modify their behavior. It's full speed ahead, no matter what, even if they're headed for the shoals.

Both kinds of awareness, *introspective* and *interpersonal,* are important. To be strong in both requires that you know what's going on inside of you, and how this bears on your thoughts, feelings, attitudes, statements, and actions; you also have to be clear about who you are as a person, what you value, and the limits beyond which you are unwilling to go, no matter what. And, you have to be able to detect, on the fly, how others are responding to you, whether what you're doing or saying is, or is not, working.

A leader who is introspective is also likely to be socially aware, and vice verse. But this is not always the case. It is possible for a person to be psychologically aware but socially obtuse, or, turning things around, socially aware but psychologically obtuse. Let's consider these two types of insight in more detail.

PSYCHODYNAMIC INSIGHT

An executive I once knew was so moody that his assistant hated to come to work. The assistant never knew what a day would bring forth, whether the executive would act like a social worker or a bounty hunter. Everything seemed to hinge on how the morning had gone with his wife, whether they had taken the dog to the vet the night before, or if their kids had been selected for roles in the school play. What made his moodiness even more troublesome was that he seemed completely unaware of the connection between what was going on at home, and therefore what was going on inside of him, and how that affected his behavior. It got so bad that, if he trudged rather than sauntered down the hall, his assistant would mutter, "The iceman cometh."[1] This executive was seriously deficient in *psychodynamic insight.*

A psychological *dynamic* is a mental process. To speak, therefore, of a person's *psychodynamics* is to refer to his or her inner workings. Such workings often involve what is only partially conscious or even unconscious. These hidden processes play themselves out in conscious thoughts, feelings, perceptions, moods, attitudes, and actions.

A person with little psychodynamic insight, therefore, is someone who is largely without awareness of such inner processes. As in the case of the executive described earlier, few if any connections are made that would enable the person to recognize why, for example, he or she is irritable, anxious, or depressed. Such an individual is by and large unable to use words to represent psychological states, beyond crudely labeling raw emotions like anger. He or she is not what those in my profession term *psychologically minded.*

Effective leaders know what's going on within them and how this potentially influences their ability to think. Clear thinking involves, at least, the capacity to do the following:

- Notice when a term is ambiguously defined.
- Draw correct inferences and notice patterns and trends.
- Detect unwarranted assumptions embedded within questions or statements.[2]
- Tell the difference between a valid and invalid deduction.
- Correctly interpret complex data sets.
- Evaluate the soundness of premises and arguments based on them.

Any one of these can be impaired by strong feelings, disruptive mood states, personal desires, corporate aspirations, or rigidly held beliefs.

Self-aware leaders know that if their thinking is impaired, their judgment is also likely to be. So, they take steps to minimize such impairment. They may, for example, delay making important decisions if they're having a bad day. Or, they may take pains to discuss options with those whose opinions are different and who are known for dispassionate analysis. Then, too, they are sensitive to anything that runs counter to their values, when for example they are being pressured to act in ways they will regret.

PSYCHOSOCIAL INSIGHT

As suggested earlier, psychodynamic insight has to do with how well you understand what's going on inside of you, and how this affects what you say and do. Psychosocial insight, on the contrary, has to do with how well you grasp what goes on between you and another person, or between you and a group. How accurately, for example, can you read their reactions?

One executive I worked with would begin a sentence that went on for twenty minutes without a break.[3] No periods, no semicolons, and few commas, to the point that I used to feel claustrophobic just listening to him. His colleagues would consult him on technical matters, since he was intelligent and knew what he was talking about, but they resorted to the written word as much as they could when they needed his advice. Rather than walking into his office, they would send an e-mail, intending to avoid his twenty-minute run-on sentences. It never once dawned on him that others shied away because of his communication patterns. He wasn't picking up the social cues.

Another executive would stubbornly march through her script, word-by-word, and worst of all slide-by-slide. Even if the CEO told her to summarize, get to the point, or skip the details, she would press on relentlessly. If there were ninety-three slides, she was steadfastly determined to get through every one of them. She, too, was missing the cues.

Finally, I recall one manager from a health care company who seemed unaware of how much his peers despised him. He was creative, well educated, and mentally agile—and more than happy to remind those around him of all three. His implicit message was, "Look how smart I am and you're not." He was arrogant, egocentric, and abrupt, all of which left others feeling demeaned, diminished, and disparaged. Like the executives described in the preceding two paragraphs, he was largely without psychosocial insight. Effective leaders are aware of their impact

An important but rarely discussed component of such awareness is the ability to imagine in advance how a particular audience is likely to respond to a given statement. Doing this is not always easy. I've given talks, hundreds of them, both to small groups and large audiences. At times, I was unable to anticipate how a given statement was going to be received, and later wished I'd expressed myself differently. Minor failures of anticipation are neither unusual nor eventful, but a leader cannot afford to make many major anticipatory mistakes. In addition to picking up how others are responding in the moment, you have to think through, ahead of time, how an audience is *likely* to respond. Is it large or small, simple or sophisticated, and will your presentation be in person, on the phone, via a videoconference, in the form of a webinar, or by e-mail?

What works in one setting, or through one communication channel, does not always work in another. Research has suggested, for example, that you can sometimes be more persuasive by phone than in person. Across situations, the level of formality will be different—typically less formal if you're addressing a small group. How much, if any, to use visual aids depends on the nature of the material to be presented; visuals must always remain *aids,* so it rarely if ever makes sense to read through slides during a talk. Finally, humor is useful—to a point. You can err on the side of being humorless and therefore dry, or on the side of sounding frivolous, which can dilute, cheapen, or trivialize your message. Attention to such details as level of formality, appropriate use of graphics, and the suitability of humor can make or break almost any speech or presentation.

UNHAPPY CONVERGENCES

Some people who lack self-insight are also devoid of social insight. They are hopelessly unrealistic about their abilities, know everything, and of course can do everything. Others may see them as decidedly less knowledgeable and capable than they see themselves. Self-conceit prevents them from deferring to others, even when doing so would make sense, or from admitting when they're wrong. Nor are they able to keep their critical opinions to themselves, when doing so would be both prudent and constructive. Although they appear confident, their surface bravado often masks a profound sense of inferiority, which they attempt to overcome by one-upping peers. They are, at root, hostile, whether subtly or overtly, and their unquenchable need to elevate their status at the expense of others is distinctly off-putting. They, therefore, lack both *psychodynamic* and *psychosocial* insight.

Other people with low self-insight are irrationally critical of themselves. They may be talented but fail to recognize this. Whatever they do is never good enough, and their quest for perfection becomes an inner demon that allows them no rest and shows them no mercy. We tend to do unto others what we do to ourselves, so those who are never satisfied with who they are or what they do can turn into tyrants. They're rarely pleased with what anyone else does either. This negativity bias distorts their perceptions and makes it hard for them to read interpersonal cues. They may become so self-absorbed that they rarely look beyond themselves enough to notice how others are reacting. They, too, lack both kinds of insight.

A NECESSARY CONDITION

Insight comes first in the list of interpersonal effectiveness facets because, directly or indirectly, the other facets depend on it. As noted earlier, unlike components of the Big Five, the facets of IE are not independent of each other. It is difficult to be skilled at self-regulation, which is what Goleman calls the second facet, if you cannot determine when it is and is not appropriate to hold back. It is also more difficult to work for anything beyond your own interests, the third facet of IE, if you're oblivious to others and their welfare. As for demonstrating that you care about them and what they're experiencing, the fourth facet, you have to be able to imagine yourself in their shoes, and being able to do this hinges on knowing yourself and how what you've gone through maps to what you perceive them to be going through. Finally, it is difficult to be convincing if you don't know what's going on inside of you and can't decipher the evaluative messages others are sending. These other four facets of IE, therefore, all depend to a considerable degree on insight.

While insight does not guarantee that you will exercise restraint, act nobly, demonstrate interpersonal sensitivity, or be persuasive, it is almost certain that, without both psychodynamic and psychosocial awareness, it will be difficult for you to do any of these well. Insight is therefore a necessary condition for IE. A leader's level of insight sets a kind of upper limit on interpersonal effectiveness.

GETTING TO KNOW YOURSELF

Pharmaceutical companies, once they have saturated the market for use of a profitable drug to ameliorate one condition, sometimes begin to cross-market it for the amelioration of others. A drug that proves effective in the treatment of depression, for example, may after a few years be advertised as reducing anxiety.[4]

Psychological services, too, are sometimes oversold, to the point that even our judicial system has sometimes inappropriately subscribed to them. Although it occasionally happens that someone who is compelled by a judge to undergo psychotherapy or counseling benefits from it, a person usually has to *want* help for either one to do much good. Psychological services are not mechanically applied treatments. Unlike an insulin injection that would do its magic whether or not the patient were even awake, psychological services have to be *voluntarily*—the person has to desire them.

If and when this is the case, they can be of noteworthy value. This is particularly true for those who have never been able to pause long enough to think much about their life histories, how they internalized the values they have, where their attitudes came from, the nature of their deeper feelings, and in general how they came to be the persons they are today.

We live in a competitive society. Given the performance demands we're up against coupled with the demands we impose on ourselves, we hardly have time to savor the aroma of a well-cooked meal. It's not unusual for people to go through college and immediately into a high-pressure job without ever having thought much about why they do what they do, act as they act, or want what they want.

Self-exploration can be a waste of time. Some people see a therapist several times a week without ever becoming serious about using the time to real advantage. When I practiced as a clinician, I had little patience with this. But, if a person sincerely wanted to engage in self-exploration, it was a different matter, and usually a fruitful one.

If you have never taken the time to talk with a psychological profes-sional, I encourage you to do so (see the Appendix for advice on how to find a practitioner). Since few people consult a therapist or counselor pri-marily to grow—most come in because of an acute symptom or distressing problem—you're likely to be an especially valued client.

FEEDBACK AS INDISPENSIBLE

The most important strategy for increasing social awareness is to seek high-quality feedback and make sure you get it. Executives tend to com-plain most about two things. The first is not having enough time for strate-gic thinking. This is no surprise, given that the average executive activity lasts about seven minutes. Days quickly fill up with short-term exigen-cies that crowd out big-picture reflection. This amounts to the tyranny of the urgent over the important. Given that an hour of thoughtful planning is worth many hours of knee-jerk execution, this complaint is certainly understandable.

Their second complaint is not getting enough feedback. The higher a person climbs in many organizations, the more that person is likely to suf-fer from the din of a deafening silence. And, the higher your position, the more vulnerable you are to receiving an unexpected *pink slip,* a term once used for a termination notice. To obtain high-quality feedback that will help you further develop your leadership skills, you will almost certainly have to seek it *actively.* It is unlikely to come to you.

Some people are *checkers.* They continually ask if they're okay, if they're doing the right thing, and so on, which makes them seem inse-cure and off balance. They're seeking reassurance more than candor and would fare better if they did less checking. Most leaders, however, worry so much about coming across as tentative that they ask for feedback far less often than they should.

Your effectiveness as a leader depends on your impact. You cannot fine-tune this impact without knowing what it is, in contrast to what you hope or imagine it to be. It is vitally important to understand how others per-ceive you, and this includes your peers as well as those above and below you. If you don't get accurate feedback, you're playing catch in the dark.

As noted in Chapter 4, the idea that organizations are run by completely rational people is simply not tenable. A lot more goes into decision mak-ing than the objective calculation of gains, loses, risks, costs, and benefits. There are misperceptions, biases, fads, feelings, and a lot more. Within any organization, whether for-profit or not-for-profit, your impact on others can affect your outcome even more than how smart or motivated you are. Some otherwise intelligent and highly motivated people are interpersonally tone-deaf. They have never come to terms with how those above them often value loyalty more than spectacular displays of brilliance. Or, how certain peers might prove disloyal, or those who today are their subordinates could tomorrow become their supervisors.

To demonstrate the value of high-quality feedback, I want to share two personal stories. Thirty years ago, after a faculty meeting, I went to lunch with another professor. I trusted her and, more or less casually, asked for feedback. Her response consisted of a single sentence: "It's obvious you can win an argument with anyone else on the faculty." This hit me so hard that I don't think I heard another word through the rest of the meal. Nor did I finish my lunch. I just sat there numb.

It was clear that she cared and wasn't trying to hurt me, which is perhaps what made her words so powerful. What she said had never occurred to me. There were twenty other professors on that faculty, most of whom were highly intelligent, and I didn't see myself as any more skilled at debate than they. Nor did I regard myself as particularly argumentative. But, obviously, that's not what my colleague saw.

I never did it again. One-trial learning. If she'd never given me that feedback, I probably would have failed as a management consultant.

The second story relates to the CEO of my largest and longest-standing corporate client and its senior vice president (SVP) of human resources. Twenty-five years ago, its CEO was vice president of human resources for one of the corporation's subsidiaries, and the SVP was a high-level HR manager. The three of us were chatting in an office, so it seemed like a good time to ask for feedback. "You have trouble letting go of the bone," they told me. Ever since, I've paid more attention to cues indicating when it's time to cease and desist. You can press an issue only so far before it starts to grate on people.[5]

Here's a third story, this one about someone else, a promising executive. At the time, she was a vice president in an operating company. Several people remarked that her first reflex would often be to ask, "What's in it for me?" We're all to some extent self-interested and self-referential. We want to know what the cost–benefit ratio is for any change that materially affects us. But, for at least three reasons, saying this out loud is not always wise.

First, coming across as overtly individualistic and therefore selfish is bad form, at least in our part of the world. It's even worse form in parts of Asia, where clan and community are highly valued and it's blatantly countercultural to lead with what's-in-it-for-me (WIFM) questions. Modern Western corporations may not function as clans but they do become tribes,[6] to the point that for many of those who work for them, they take on something akin to religious significance. Not to put the welfare of the corporate tribe first can become a kind of heresy, a road to secular excommunication.

Second, as we'll address in Chapter 13, nobility of motivation counts. Few of us are drawn to those who are excessively self-seeking, and if we work for an organization in whose mission we believe, we want to think of our colleagues as equally committed to that mission—more than to their next raise, bonus, or promotion. Selfish people do not impress us as trustworthy colleagues who can be counted on to take personal risks when it counts; we see them as more likely to engage in CYA[7] behavior when the waters begin to churn.

Finally, what first comes out of a person's mouth may not accurately reflect that person's deeper motives. An individual can impress colleagues as more WIFM-oriented, simply because of what he or she spontaneously says, than another who is actually far more so. This, I believe, was the case with this executive.

She was a bright and intuitive person. We'd spent many hours in conversation, and I was consistently impressed with how insightful she was. This woman could read the culture and the actors who shaped it as well if not better than anyone else in the company. Despite this high degree of social awareness, however, there was a blind spot. She was simply unaware of how her self-references were hurting her. Because she was unusually talented, I suspect she thought it was only reasonable to ask, now and then, how the corporation intended to treat her—what her next assignment would be. Yet, raising such issues as straightforwardly as she'd been doing was not working.

Since it's my job to help high-potential leaders become more effective, I invited her to lunch one day and raised the subject. She was astute, so I didn't have to tell her twice. Neither I nor anyone else to my knowledge ever heard her raise another WIFM issue. Like most of us, she continued to care about her progress, but she stopped asking direct questions about it, and instead found other ways to check on her future prospects. She wisely elected to trust that the corporation would treat her fairly, which in turn prompted it to trust her with increasingly greater responsibilities. She eventually became COO of one of its telecommunications subsidiaries.

I chose this particular example to demonstrate how even minor changes in awareness can make a tremendous difference. This woman was relatively selfless. She'd make any sacrifice required of her for the good of the enterprise. But that's not how she was coming across. At senior levels of organizations, as in some Olympic events, winning the gold can be a matter of millimeters. A small adjustment can affect the outcome.

Leaders can fail either because they refuse to seek feedback or because they ignore the feedback they get. Norman Vincent Peale had it right: "The trouble with most of us is that we would rather be ruined by praise than saved by criticism." One manager I knew was promoted to vice president because an influential senior executive was impressed by his diligence and expertise. When he moved into his new job, he became a harsh taskmaster who was on the brink of triggering an outright rebellion among his direct reports. I suggested that he collect feedback about his impact by launching an electronic *360*. A 360 is a tool for gathering anonymous ratings and comments from those north (supervisors), south (subordinates), and east and west (peers)—hence the compass label. The e-mail I sent him containing the link to begin the process sat in his inbox for months. Either he didn't believe the feedback would be accurate, it wouldn't be worth the time to gather, or he didn't need it. Like others we've discussed, he left to pursue other interests.

We have already met another executive in Chapter 4, the well-credentialed one who was a vice president for a leading company in its industry. You may recall that, on his behalf, I collected feedback from his co-workers. They reported that he failed to make connections between strategies and tactics, needed to stop flitting from one idea to the next, and got lost in the stratosphere of higher theoretical thinking. In that chapter, I never finished the story, which was that I presented him with the feedback and offered concrete suggestions for how he could become a more effective leader. None of it seemed to register. He, too, was eventually asked to resign.

"Beware of anyone asking for feedback." This proverb is often repeated because when many people ask for feedback, they actually want reassurance or flattery. Since people generally know this, if you want high-quality feedback, not only do you have to ask for it, but you also have to convince those you ask that you truly want to hear it. If you manage to persuade them, they are likely to tell you at least a few things that sting. Keep in mind that a lot of the best lessons we learn involve pain, such as not to touch hot stoves or change lanes without looking. The trick is to interpret criticism as constructive coaching.

Don't wait for such guidance to come up in your appraisal. By that time, it may be too late. Moreover, it—whatever *it* happens to be—may not come up at all. Depending on who your supervisor is, you may never hear what you most need to. If the three rules for buying a house are location, location, and location, the three rules for obtaining feedback are ask, ask, and ask again.

I'd like to share three questions that I use in one form or another for a wide variety of purposes. They are simple, but if you don't rush in with chatter that cuts off the conversation, they can unearth a tremendous amount of helpful information.

1. What am I doing well—what should I keep doing, or do even more of?
2. What could or should I be doing better—what might I do less of, or do differently?
3. What two or three concrete/actionable recommendations would you make in the interest of my becoming a more effective leader?

Try using them. You may be surprised by how much they yield. Bring a notebook with you when you do. Write it down, all of it. We forget much of what we learn within twenty-four hours, and nearly all of it within a month.

The quality of the feedback you obtain is going to depend on whom you ask and under what circumstances. It makes no sense to ask only those who are going to cater to you, rather than saying what they think. Nor does it make sense to ask those with little insight, such as colleagues who are not psychosocially astute. And, although asking rivals for feedback can sometimes be more useful than asking friends, it may not always make sense to ask your fiercest competitors. Choose only those you know to be both observant and benevolent.

THE VALUE OF SKIP-LEVEL INTERVIEWS

It is sometimes possible to learn quite a bit about your indirect impact—your influence through immediate subordinates—by conducting skip-level interviews. These are structured conversations you have with employees who report to your direct reports. If, for example, Mark Johnson reports directly to you, and Pat Smith reports to Mark Johnson, the interview would be with Pat Smith. Here are a series of questions relating to such interviews, along with the answers.

What is the value of conducting skip-level interviews? Their primary virtue is that they enable you to obtain high-quality information for use in the developmental coaching of subordinates. They can also help you learn about how you are affecting those within your larger sphere of influence.

What new information might I obtain from skip-level interviews? How a subordinate relates to you may be different from how he or she relates to those at lower levels in the organization. Some people *work up* beautifully but are less effective in relating to, or leading, those below them. Hence, the snide epithet, "Kiss up, kick down."

How should a skip-level interview be structured? It is best to allow 30–45 minutes for the interview, which should be conducted, if possible, face to face. Tell them you'll treat the information as confidential (see later). Use a small number of open-ended questions (again see later) and encourage the other person to talk; avoid rushing in to fill the silences. If anything remains unclear, *say it back* to the person you are interviewing, and ask for confirmation. Take good notes.

Who should be interviewed? In the ideal, you would interview all of your indirect (once-removed) reports, in other words, all employees who report directly to your immediate subordinates. Doing this, however, may require more time than you have. If so, here are some ways to reduce the amount of time required: (1) Limit each interview to between twenty and thirty minutes; (2) Spread the interviews over a two- or three-month period; (3) Interview only some of those who report to each of your direct reports; or, (4) Enlist the help of a trusted interviewer to act on your behalf (either in-house senior staff or a reputable outside consultant).

If you use the third option, it would be prudent to include (a) the person likely to be the most positive, (b) the one likely to have the most critical feedback, and (c) someone who is likely to be somewhere in the middle. If you use the fourth option, choose this person or persons carefully, with a special eye on potential negativity (mountains out of molehills) or positivity (molehills out of mountains) biases.

What are the rules of the road? When you conduct skip-level interviews, you are asking people to put themselves at risk. This is because of the consequential relationships that exist between them and their supervisors. Whatever information you collect, therefore, should be "on the record" (used) but "not for attribution" (anonymous). If it is not possible to use a piece of information without revealing its source, especially when the information is negative, don't use it, regardless of how valuable it might be in coaching. Confidentiality has to be honored.

What should I listen for during the interview? Leadership, at the most basic level, has to do with *impact* and *influence*. And these, in turn, depend on how a leader is *perceived*. Listen carefully for recurring themes. A well-conducted skip-level interview may provide you with a wealth of information about the extent to which your subordinate exhibits the following four kinds of leadership[8]:

- General   Inspiring others and getting things done through them
- Informational   Sharing useful information about the company and its priorities
- Competitional   Striving to perform well and succeed in the marketplace
- Relational   Fostering morale and a positive work environment

You may also pick up information that you can use to help immediate subordinates in one or more domains of the Big Five.

How should I present the information to subordinates? Although you may need more or less time with a particular subordinate, a one-hour meeting is usually about right for presenting feedback obtained via skip-level interviews. Emphasize that you have asked for perceptions, which may or may not mirror reality. But also point out that perceptions reflect impact, and that part of a leader's job is to have a productive impact. Stress how "this information is for you"—because it is. And, of course, highlight positive feedback. Strive to be a coach rather than a critic.

What makes a good skip-level interview? A skip-level interview can be a complete waste of time, an incredibly rich source of information, or anything in between. The two keys to success are (1) *establishing trust* and (2) *listening carefully* without biasing those interviewed.

What specific questions might I ask? Although everyone has his or her own interviewing style, the following questions usually work well; note how all three focus on concrete behaviors rather than general characteristics. They directly parallel those I suggested you use to gather feedback on yourself.

1. What does [Name] do well—what are his/her strengths and assets?
2. What could or should [Name] do better—what are his/her developmental needs?
3. If you were to coach [Name], what two or three specific (behavioral) recommendations would you make to help improve his/her performance?

Each of your direct reports may have additional questions that he or she would like you to ask. If time permits, these can be worked out collaboratively before you begin the interviews.

PROVIDING FEEDBACK TO OTHERS

Caring and candor characterize all good relationships. Without caring, you have thinly veiled brutality: "I'm only being honest." Without candor, you end up with a watery broth without nutritional value. Both need to be present if you want your feedback to be constructive.

Many times I've taken the risk of providing feedback that could have resulted in my termination. Guess what? It's never happened. Not only that, but each time I took such a risk the person in relation to whom I took it valued me even more for having had the necessary courage. The worth of my stock actually went up. People almost always appreciate honest feedback if they know you're trying to help them, if your heart is good. To borrow a slogan from the Army, help others be all they can be. Go out of your way to accommodate their requests for feedback and coaching.

MENTORS, COACHES, AND SPONSORS

You need people to play three different but potentially overlapping roles in your career: mentor, coach, and sponsor. All three can be valuable sources of guidance. A *mentor,* usually older, is someone who shows you the ropes, tries to keep you from stepping on landmines, and helps you benefit from his or her experience, especially mistakes. A *coach,* as in athletics, is someone who helps you play a better game. This person can see you from the outside and therefore offer an additional set of eyes and ears. A *sponsor* is someone who either promotes your interests and advocates for you, or who's on the way up and takes you along for the ride.

Without a mentor or two, you're going to make unnecessary and avoidable errors. Absent a good coach, who might or might not be a colleague, it will be harder to fine-tune your game. And if you don't have at least one sponsor, you may top out, never again to advance in your organization. As in our discussion of networking in Chapter 7, it is dangerous to try to manipulate people into playing any of these roles.

The easiest way to recruit a mentor or coach is simply to ask. It's flattering to be asked for advice, and if you ask someone to mentor or coach you, it is that person's advice you're seeking. As discussed in Chapter 4, "I need your help" can be a compellingly powerful statement. Getting someone to be your sponsor can be more difficult, and the best way to do this is consistently to exceed expectations.

Strive to improve on all dimensions of the Big Five. Remember $P = A \times M$, so pay particular attention to the contents of Chapters 4 and 6. Work to improve your IE as well. No one wants to be associated with someone who is chronically rude, interpersonally dense, out to lunch, impulsive, without compassion, or unpersuasive. To be emotionally intelligent is to be more, rather than less, socially attractive. For someone to sponsor you, they have to be willing to entrust you with more responsibility or at least encourage others to do so.

I'll end this chapter with a bit of practical advice. If you want to get promoted, have the good sense to talk, dress, and act like those one level above you. How exactly to do this will vary from company to company and culture to culture.

Although senior leaders in some organizations might be reluctant to admit it, they will promote to senior positions only those who appear to be in their elevated social class and who correspondingly speak with textbook grammar—"Everything's going *good*" will not cut it. Such leaders will probably also be attuned to academic pedigree. At the opposite extreme, certain senior leaders might stigmatize anyone who comes across as scholarly, stuffy, or pedantic. They are on the lookout for those who, regardless of gender, fail metaphorically to establish themselves as *regular guys* or *one of the boys.*[9]

However those above you behave, try to follow their lead unless it runs counter to your ethics. Wear suits or jackets if they do, and casual clothes if they don't. In just about every company, except perhaps those that take pride in high-level managers picking up wrenches, keep your hair combed and your fingernails clean and trimmed; care of the hands is a definite social marker.

People vote for those they perceive to be like them, who reflect and personify their values. If your personal preferences, whether high- or lowbrow, do not match the ethos of the organization in which you find yourself, think seriously about working in and for another one.

TWELVE

Restraint: Impulse Control and Self-Monitoring

Can you regulate what you say and do, and so keep yourself from instantly blurting out what you think? Are you able to pick the right time and place to express yourself? Do you govern the communication of your moods and emotions, or can others quickly sense your frustration, impatience, displeasure, intolerance, or anger? Can you keep your cool under pressure?

A Latin proverb goes, "It is absurd that a man should rule others, who cannot rule himself." Few qualities are as central to effective leadership as restraint, the ability to regulate the immediate and counterproductive expression of thoughts, feelings, and attitudes. Such expressions can range from spontaneous criticism, disapproval, and disdain to irritation, anger, and rage. Organizations don't run well when there's low morale or unnecessary friction. Demoralization and friction can cause damage, and if these become intense and prolonged, they are capable of causing the organization to slow down and, in the extreme, stall. This is why good leaders don't allow themselves to become unwitting victims of temporary mood states. People will tend to trust you more if they perceive that you can harness self-expression and not lash out merely because it feels good or lets you get it out of your system.

Stress, it has been quipped, is when your mind has to restrain your body from choking the daylights out of someone who deserves it. Think about the last time you were in a meeting with some less-than-gifted soul who frustrated you by stubbornly clinging to an absurd position and, worse, lacked the good sense to realize it. You might have been tempted to explode. If you resisted the temptation, you demonstrated *impulse control.*

Certain people have such defective impulse control that it takes little stress to detonate them. They have what those in the missile business call a fast rise time, and so spew forth whatever they think or feel, regardless of impact. Some of these individuals are oblivious to the effects of their outbursts. Others are aware of how their words and actions affect others, but they cannot control the expression of either. They may go to sleep at night wishing they'd said or done something differently. But a new day brings with it a fresh opportunity for another outburst, and it's not long before one comes. Their need for emotional ventilation is so prepossessing that they simply cannot resist or suppress it. They become victims of what Goleman calls *emotional hijacking.* People who are prone to such hijacking are quick to voice displeasure and disapproval, and they may not hesitate to argue with or correct their supervisors. Those around them may wonder about their maturity, wisdom, and sense of decorum, and they may know this. But their behavior doesn't change.

Insufficient restraint can be career limiting because wounds to the egos of others may be long remembered, even in the most rough-and-tumble organization. Those you cause to lose face today may cause you to lose rank tomorrow. Robots do not run organizations, people do. And as humans, we have no end of pride to nourish and no dearth of self-esteem to protect, even at the expense of bottom-line results.

FAILURES OF SELF-DISCIPLINE

I have run across some glaring failures of self-restraint, each of which inflicted significant damage on an enterprise. Here are three of the more memorable ones:

1. Because of internal friction and discord, a thriving partnership lost its place as the dominant firm in its industry.
2. An entrepreneur derailed the company he founded by resorting to a draconian way of building alignment—he simply fired anyone who voiced an opinion that differed from his.
3. A CEO, against all advice, impulsively sold off a core business and nearly bankrupted the profitable parent company he led.

All three of these examples were rooted in failures of restraint: the first in lack of expressive control, so that the partnership degenerated, initially into covert war and eventually into open combat; the second in not being able to resist the temptation to suppress dissent, so that its leader doomed himself to a kind of autocratic fantasyland; and, the third by knee-jerk corporate myopia that overrode good judgment. Countless failures of restraint occur inside the walls of for-profit corporations, and the annual cost to shareholders probably runs into the billions. The same impulse-control problems occur in government and corporate nonprofits, and the resulting costs to society are no doubt staggering.

I should add, in passing, that regardless of how frustrated or unhappy you become in your job, never threaten to quit—an obvious failure of self-control. Issuing this threat implies low frustration tolerance, fickleness, and instability. It also suggests disloyalty and invites the person you're threatening to take you up on your offer. Most important of all, it's implied. Unless you're in the armed forces, you can always resign. In threatening resignation, you gain nothing and potentially pay a significant price.

This also seems like the place to point out that, except in rare instances of gross incompetence, malfeasance, or mental derangement, the burden is at least 60 percent on you to get along with your supervisor. I have no hard evidence for this—certainly no stone tablets—but to me it seems self-evident by virtue of the nature of organizational life. Recall our discussion in Chapter 5 of how dysfunctional friction is.

SENDING THE RIGHT MESSAGES

We have already noted that whenever we are in the presence of another person or group, whether face to face or via an electronic medium such as videoconferencing or e-mail, we are teaching that person or group how to perceive us, and how to act in relation to us. This is even true of handwritten notes and letters, though fewer and fewer people use them. It is therefore prudent to keep the following realities in mind.

No one wants to be around an erratic leader who might pop off at any moment, perhaps overreacting to some minor deficiency or breach of protocol. If you blow up at one person, you might just as easily blow up at someone else, and subordinates will worry they might be next. There is little if anything more important to fostering trust in your character than demonstrating that you can restrain yourself, especially when letting it fly would be ever so satisfying. Nor is there much that is more central to fostering trust in your competence. The world within any organization is indeed a stage. If a leader does not demonstrate restraint while performing on it, how can subordinates be confident that he or she will exercise self-discipline when confronting a tempting but imprudent opportunity?

If as a leader you develop a reputation for punishing people for minor infractions, and fly off the handle at whatever displeases you, you will induce fear. Some wariness by subordinates may be desirable. As a leader, you have to insist that others occasionally do unpleasant things like working late or on weekends, which in the absence of consequences they might not choose to do. It is therefore good for subordinates to know you mean business. If, however, you rule more by intimidation than inspiration, those reporting to you may well learn not to disappoint you, but they will also learn, when they can get away with it, *not* to tell you what you don't want to hear. This is a precarious position in which to place yourself. Subordinates and peers will come to regard you as a dangerous person and, so, will no longer trust you. Nor will you be able to trust them, regardless of how they act in your presence—no matter how fawning, solicitous, or seemingly loyal. Those you've intimidated into submission might even turn on you if they have a chance.

A SPECIAL CHALLENGE WOMEN FACE

The English anthropologist and linguist Gregory Bateson introduced the concept of the *double bind* in the 1950s. It refers to the dilemma that occurs when a person is given contradictory messages or commands; the individual cannot comply with both at the same time. To follow one injunction is not to follow the other.

To advance in an organization, executives and managers typically have to demonstrate determination. This implies the willingness to mete out consequences, to back up directives. When subordinates do what's expected, they are rewarded, but when they don't, they either go unrewarded ("No raise for you this year") or are punished ("We're going to have to let you go"). Any leader, male or female, has to be willing to use force, to act aggressively. We can pretend there's a clear line between assertion and aggression, and that a leader can invariably avoid crossing that line, but this, as we have seen, is wishful thinking. The intentional infliction of pain or injury on another person, in the service of having one's wishes carried out, is aggression. Always was and always will be.

A leader has to be perceived as willing to use power to foster compliance and deter noncompliance. In the face of failures to perform, this power may take the form of social avoidance or ostracism, as it might in *totally* volunteer organizations whose leaders may conclude, in their more discouraged moments, that they have ended up herding cats or stacking marbles. In other organizations, profit or nonprofit, it may entail material consequences, such as passing someone over for promotion or not granting a raise or a bonus.

A man who expresses himself forcefully is likely to be perceived as a strong leader, but a woman who similarly expresses herself may be perceived as harsh and unfeeling. Or, worse, as riding to work on a broom. When was the last time you heard a male executive or manager referred to as a warlock? This is slowly changing, but forcefulness in a woman still tends to be judged more harshly than it is in a man. Unless she's the CEO, therefore, she has to be considerably more artful in how she uses power and in how careful she is about appearing to remain, at least most of the time, on the assertion part of the assertion–aggression continuum. Artful, in this context, often means less direct and more oblique. This is not fair to women. But, in many organizations, it is the reality.

CULTIVATING RESTRAINT BY MONITORING EXPRESSIVE BEHAVIOR

In the early 1970s, a doctoral student at Stanford did his dissertation on what he labeled the self-monitoring of expressive behavior (SMEB). Self-monitoring turns out to be key to how people act when they're with others; his dissertation spawned over 2,000 research studies. The SMEB has to do with the size of the gap between one's private and public selves. Some people freely express what they think and feel, regardless of who's around, while others carefully adjust their self-expression in response to social context.

People high on self-monitoring are concerned about the impressions they make on others, and they have the ability to manage these impressions. Consider a couple of the true–false items on the scale that measures SMEB. One is, *I have trouble changing my behavior to suit different people and different situations.* Those high on self-monitoring answer *false* to it, while those low on self-monitoring answer *true.* Another is, *I would not change my opinions (or the way I do things) in order to please someone or win their favor.* Again, those high on self-monitoring respond *false,* while those low on self-monitoring respond *true.*

The eighteen items on this scale can be sorted into three groups or clusters. The first has to do with *expressive self-control,* the ability to manage what you convey to others about what's going on inside of you. The second has to do with *social stage presence,* the tendency to perform in social situations. And, the third is called *other-directed self-presentation,* which has to do with acting in ways that others want or expect.

Basic social skill requires that we compute the likely impact of what we say and do. At one end of the SMEB scale is the person who does no self-editing. This is the one who says everything that comes to mind, without organizing it so it's coherent, and who acts on every impulse. This is a pretty good sidewalk definition of psychosis, of living in a world of one's own. Think of those who talk to themselves in public, disregard the residual rules of society, and may even assault people verbally or physically. Residual rules are those that everyone comes to understand simply by living in a particular culture. Little or no formal instruction is needed. In Western society, for example, it is considered impolite to belch loudly at the table, whereas in certain regions of the Far East, it is considered impolite not to.

At the other end of the scale are two kinds of people who are strikingly high on self-monitoring. One is the person who says or does nothing without first calculating how this is likely to achieve opportunistic ends. Such is the sociopath, exemplified in Patricia Highsmith's 1955 psychological thriller, *The Talented Mr. Ripley* (made into a film in 1999). Empathy is in shockingly short supply.

The other is the superficial person, sometimes described as an empty suit. This is the one who has no discernible core or center, and little in the way of an identity beyond simple conformity and blending in. Such a hollow soul will express a fan's love of baseball to a sports fanatic, and five minutes later tell someone who detests the game how much he or she also loathes it.

There is sometimes a fine line between social skill and interpersonal manipulation. The side of the line you fall on in any encounter often depends on your motives. We are complex social beings, and any time we interact with someone else, several motives may come into play, some altruistic and others not. If, in using whatever charm you have, your principal aim is simply to enjoy and encourage a mutually satisfying and productive relationship, this qualifies as social skill. A certain amount of such skill is required for human transactions to proceed smoothly. If, on the contrary, your fundamental aim is predatory, to extract something of material or social value from the other person by using some form of deception, this is manipulation. Most encounters within an organization are instrumental but not predatory.

If you blurted out everything you thought, you wouldn't get very far in any organization. You'd also end up with few friends. Yet, if you never shared what you were thinking and feeling, others would be unable to relate to you, to connect. They would find you cold, distant, and lacking in humanity. Neither extreme of self-monitoring, therefore, is likely to foster trust. When it comes to self-disclosure, it's good to have not too much and not too little, to follow Aristotle's principle of the *golden mean* by occupying the middle ground between excess and deficit.

HARNESSING EMOTIONALITY

How you're tempted to respond in the moment may not be what, with a bit more reflection, you'd say or do. So, it is a good idea to let your feelings age. Just a few weeks ago, I was talking with someone in a high-pressure job. Although the problem had been fixed, he was verbalizing the desire to have it out with a colleague who, through negligence, had almost caused him to wait several extra days to board a flight home. He'd been away for weeks and sorely missed his family. "Don't do it!" I said, adding, "It only takes one misstep to be sidelined. Let it pass. You can always fall back on the political motto, forgive and remember."

One way to let your feelings age is to write them out without holding back. Just make sure that no one else lays hands or eyes on what you write. Allow it get cold. In a day or two, read what you've written, and think about whether the long-term consequences of unfiltered expression are worth the short-term satisfactions. You may decide they're not.

All through Plato's dialogues, we encounter the Socratic method. Plato's usual protagonist is his teacher Socrates, who rarely claims to know the answer to a question. He merely analyzes answers advanced by others. Asking the right questions remains among the most powerful techniques for leading others to the best answer. Taking the time to come up with good questions can also have the admirable benefit of slowing you down.

As trial attorneys know, questions can be powerful. Within a corporate context, asking the right questions in a calm, respectful, but assertive manner is almost always useful, since it can help everyone involved arrive at the right conclusion and make the best decision. And if they don't, you can always ask more questions. I know one CEO who long ago developed this technique into an art form. Questioning can be a wonderful aid to learning and self-control. It's almost always superior to hostile confrontation.

Leaders, as noted earlier, are forever on stage. There is no such thing as being off duty, including and perhaps especially at an organization's social events. Those above, parallel to, and below you are continually watching. This is not designed to make you paranoid, but rather to emphasize that others cannot help noticing how you act when the context is less formal and your guard may be down. The more sinister among them may even be waiting to find something to use against you. It is therefore important to regulate your emotions at such events. Say nothing you don't want published on the organization's website.

Without much, if any, awareness of what they're doing, people unconsciously search for clues that will help them determine how much they can trust their leaders. It's important, therefore, that you keep in mind that, when it comes to a work setting or even a setting where you'll encounter fellow employees, you're always *on*. As one executive told me happened to him, you might even run into a fellow employee in an airport of a distant state; that employee will automatically take note of how you act.

It is also important to pay no unnecessary social prices. I made this recommendation in Chapter 5 and reiterated it in Chapter 8, but I want to repeat it once more here, since it stands as a critically important guideline for thriving in an organization. If someone injures you, your natural tendency may be to return the favor. This, however, is almost always unwise, because if you restrain yourself, the person who wronged you may do something later to make up for it.

A year after I joined the faculty of a training program for clinical psychologists, I was assigned to teach the course in adult psychotherapy, considered by many of the other professors to be the plum of the curriculum. At the end of my first year teaching that course, some graduate students complained, with the result that the following year a more senior professor replaced me.

This, predictably, was a wound to my self-esteem, and I was tempted to voice my objection to the dean for having caved in to student pressure. Fortunately, a psychoanalyst on the faculty advised me to refrain from protesting, to "allow the guilt to build up." He was in essence saying, "Let him stay in the position of having to make amends for having injured you—he's in your debt. But, if you discharge that debt by forcing him to absorb your anger, he will owe you nothing." I followed his advice and a year later I was reinstated. There were no further rebellions, and I continued to teach that course, to enthusiastic reviews, until I left the faculty years later.

I had a related experience with a social psychologist. Once, during a faculty meeting, a colleague asked me to do something—I can't recall what—and I responded with something along the lines of, "Don't you see how much I'm already doing?" Afterward, the social psychologist quietly asked, "What was the point? You could have handled that better. There was no upside." What he meant was that, when you offend someone, he or she is likely to have a score to settle. Fortunately, the colleague I'd rebuffed was a friend, but it could have been different. There's rarely an advantage to rudeness.

Sometimes, you know you're right but others fail to appreciate the genius of your insight. When you believe this to be the case, it can prove difficult to be patient. So, especially when you're right, or think you are, it's important to exercise self-regulation. I've been in this position many times, and it took me a while to figure out that I had to engage in *time-selling*. As noted in Chapter 8, this means raising the idea again and again. Not giving up. But, you have to be sensitive to whether you're becoming annoying. It's rarely a good idea to make the same suggestion more than once or twice in a short period. If it's not time-critical, you may enjoy the luxury of trying to sell it over the course of years. This may feel like an eternity, but it's better than training your audience to tense up when they see you coming.

You cannot expect every good idea you have to be adopted. It's important, therefore, to take the long-range view. Many consultants become frustrated because they don't see their recommendations implemented. This rarely bothers me. I'll still press an issue if I think it's important, either with an individual or organization, but I do so with the clear realization that I'm an advisor rather than a decision maker. It's their company, not mine. What I most care about is gaining a hearing, which requires access, and I will only have access if my batting average for making sound recommendations is high. The same applies to you. Establish a reputation for wisdom and patience, and bear in mind that those above you have the right to ignore your advice and override your decisions.

AVOIDING THE MISTAKE OF DE-POSITIONING THOSE ABOVE YOU

It rarely if ever makes sense to make a senior leader look bad. This is an implication of appropriately monitoring expressive behavior; it's a kind of special case. Be careful not to embarrass or de-position high-ranking leaders if you can at all help it. And, high-ranking or not, try not to de-position your boss.

When I was relatively new to consulting, the head of a company invited me to attend his two-day executive off-premises conference. An eminent business professor facilitated the first day, which went predictably well. One of the company's vice presidents facilitated the second day, which was not going well at all. I suffered more with every passing minute and kept thinking, *Get this guy off the stage!* He seemed clueless about what he was doing, or even what he was supposed to be doing.

At 10:00 A.M., we took a break and I walked into the hall. Another vice president, for whom I'd already done some work and with whom I'd established a warm relationship, strolled over. "You'd better start playing poker," he whispered. I took him to mean that, if I didn't learn to suppress my expression of displeasure, and fast, I wasn't going to be there; my consulting career with that company would be over. Having gone to a military academy, I should have realized that it's always bad form and sometimes politically dangerous to make an officer look bad, and this man was a corporate officer. I reentered the room with no displeasure on my face.

CALIBRATING YOUR IMPACT

Psychologist John Gottman of the University of Washington suggested that since people react more negatively to loss than positively to gain—it's more painful to lose $1,000 than pleasurable to gain the same amount—positive interactions must generally outnumber negative ones by a ratio of five to one. This is certainly true for marriages. Gottman knows what he's talking about. He's demonstrated the ability to predict marital dissolution simply by watching videotapes of couples talking.

In a business context, where relationships do not enjoy the conjugal adhesives of sex and affection, you should probably raise Gottman's ratio to six or seven to one. This, of course, is only a rough guideline, since it treats all gains and losses as equivalent, which they most definitely are not. The right word of praise to a subordinate, for example in response to something of which he or she is proud, may be worth more than ten or twenty nonspecific compliments. This is also true of criticisms, which like praise can differ markedly in their effects.

Because it's important to praise more than criticize, you may have to inhibit some of your perfectionistic impulses. A certain measure of exactness is probably what got you to where you are—you want things done well. If, however, the critique you're about to deliver relates to something trivial, carefully weigh the benefits of correction against the costs of demoralization.

We've already noted how CEOs tend to underestimate the impact of what they say and do. What subordinates experience as a nuclear explosion, the CEO may perceive as but a firecracker. The same underestimation principle applies at all levels of an organization. Even if the enterprise is structured in some alternative way, perhaps as a hub and spoke, matrix, or series of concentric circles, those with more power are likely to underestimate the impact of their utterances and actions on those with less power.

In whatever position you occupy, subordinates will be inclined to perceive what you say and do as more impactful than you do. So, remember that, on a scale from 1 to 10, a 3 to you may be a 7 or 8 to them. As a way to keep this disparity in mind, consider entering something along the lines of "3 to me, 8 to them" as a periodic reminder in your private calendar, say once a month. Doing this may be tedious, but it may help just to see it once in a while as you glance at your schedule. For some hapless subordinates, of course, an 8 to you is a 3 to them.

One good use of the written word is to use it to fine-tune your efforts at calibration. I've often made this recommendation to leaders who are serious about becoming more effective: write it down. We touched on this idea in Chapter 10. Whenever you have any kind of interchange that requires restraint, record it in a logbook. You might make a few brief notes about a conversation in which you became irritated, or how you reacted to a long meeting that went nowhere and accomplished little. Keep a record of what happened, what you did, and whether you were pleased with the outcome. Such record keeping will pay off. Not everyone to whom I've made this suggestion followed it, but those who did made faster and more significant progress.

CHALLENGING DILEMMAS

Depending on circumstance, you might find yourself in one of two quandaries, both of which can call on you for special restraint. The first is exemplified by what I call the *staff dilemma* and the second by what I think of as the *leader's dilemma.* If your organization has given you the responsibility to uphold standards, there may be times when you will not be able to dole out seven positives for every negative, not and remain credible. The same may be true if you supervise subordinates whose performance is deficient.

Let's first consider the staff dilemma. All staff organizations have two duties that sometimes stand in tension. The first is to serve the line divisions or departments, and in the process to retain their goodwill. Goodwill is important because staff units need line support. It's crucial to keep the channels of communication open. If you're staff, you don't want line organizations circumventing standards you're charged with upholding, or failing to talk with you about compliance difficulties. The other duty of a staff organization is to enforce those very standards, whether these relate to accounting and finance, law and regulatory affairs, human resources and personnel management, environmental stewardship and the handling of hazardous materials, engineering and construction, or something else. Staff organizations bear the responsibility *not* to allow the rules, protocols, or guidelines of the larger organization to be disregarded, much less flouted. They therefore have a certain policing function. It is not always easy to fulfill both duties at the same time, to maintain goodwill and enforce standards. High levels of IE are often required.

The leader's dilemma is similar. Nearly all leaders experience it at one time or another, and usually more than once. If you're supervising a star, someone with considerable ability, motivation, and maturity, is collegial, and knows when to lead and when to follow, there is no tension and no dilemma. And, if the employee's performance is truly abysmal, you would no doubt easily rise to the challenge, and the poor performer would soon depart. The problem arises with subordinates who are neither stars nor slackers, those who muddle along and rarely, if ever, fully apply themselves.

When supervising a marginal performer, you're sometimes caught between two conflicting duties. One is to get the best performance you can out of the person you're supervising, which usually requires keeping up that person's morale. You want the individual to be positively motivated. Your other duty is to provide him or her with candid feedback, including but not limited to what you enter into the formal appraisal. This duty is especially important because the organization's human resources department needs accurate records. It is not always easy to buoy up a marginal performer's morale while, at the same time, honoring your duty to evaluate performance honestly.

The leader's dilemma spawns much of the frustration human resources professionals live with every day. Although conflict avoidance by supervisors plays its part in the glittering generalities that fill countless personnel files, the larger part is probably attributable to the inherent tension between the two duties, between sustaining morale and truthfully evaluating negative performance. This tension mostly goes unrecognized, and if it is recognized, it's rarely discussed.

Despite the fact that mediocre workers make it hard, if not impossible, to implement the seven-to-one rule, it's almost always a good idea to praise as much as you sincerely can, and avoid harsh or demoralizing treatment of those you lead. To be effective, the praise must be authentic. If it isn't, you will lose respect and may earn some derision by coming across as amateurishly applying a canned management technique. Try to perfect the art of the sincere compliment. And, always provide honest feedback and candid documentation of performance.[1]

REMAINING POSITIVE AND OPTIMISTIC

I once knew a manager who, whenever I'd ask how he was doing, would respond with a grin and say, "Fantastic!" This went on for years. Finally, someone explained what he was doing. Here's the principle he had in mind: *It may be bullshit, but you say fantastic!* This is known as the *fantastic bullshit* rule, and it can prove useful. He was actually a happy man who worked for an excellent company, and I do not for one moment believe that he classified much of what he did as undesirable or silly. But he'd adopted this one-word response to keep himself on a positive trajectory.

Never let adversity define your reality. An important reason for reframing adversity as opportunity is that doing so will substantially decrease or eliminate any temptation you have to share your discontent. By *not* expressing negativity you don't impose a burden on others to take care of you, to fix you, a burden they may quickly come to resent. Avoiding the expression of displeasure does not mean refusing to acknowledge disappointment. You ought to acknowledge it, lest you come across as oblivious or dim-witted. But, you need to do it in a way that conveys, "I'm in for the whole tour, and you can count on me, no matter what. Let's move on." Don't let yourself get caught up in or derailed by circumstances over which you have little or no control. Refuse to expend your time and energy on what are sometimes called *gravity issues or conditions,* realities that aren't going to change.

Relatively few people who've worked inside an organization have avoided setbacks. The careers of many leaders conform to a kind of sine wave, with recurring peaks and valleys. They're in favor now, out of favor later, and then the cycle repeats. If you're in the military, the command you desired and believed you were going to get may, at the last minute, have been given to someone else. Or, if you work in a commercial enterprise, the large project you'd assumed would be yours was assigned to a political darling child, someone sprinkled with pixie dust. And, if you work in a not-for-profit enterprise, an outsider with inferior qualifications may have been installed in a post that, after years of loyal and competent service, should have been yours. The wise move is to take the setback in stride and assume that, sooner or later, if you continue to act conscientiously, everything will work out equitably. More often than not, this will be the case.

I recall sitting at breakfast one morning with a vice president who'd been reassigned from a job he loved to one that felt to him like a demotion. For some reason, hockey came to mind, and I found myself saying, "Stay on the ice. I know you feel like you're in the penalty box. But, *this too will pass,* and until it does, keep skating." This was my attempt to counter any tendency he might have had to sit on the bench. It's natural to retreat and even to withdraw when we feel hurt and unappreciated. We may have fantasies of mentally checking out, no longer caring, or even resigning. Such detachment rarely goes unnoticed. It can set in motion a self-fulfilling prophecy. We expect to be further disparaged and, so, act in ways that make this more likely. Fortunately, the vice president decided to continue skating. He retired years later in a job he loved.

Here's another story from military school. There were three one-month-long rotations of cadet officers before the permanent officers were installed in December for the rest of the year. The events I'm about to describe occurred near the end of the second rotation and involved a company commander, one of the top five officers in the battalion.

One Saturday, he and three other cadets left the grounds on liberty. They had to be back by 2130 hours (9:30 P.M.). Realizing they were going to be late, they made some bad decisions. Because of these decisions, all four suffered serious consequences. The company commander was busted, stripped of all status and power; he went from being one of the senior officers in a battalion of 300 to not much more than a plebe. But he, too, kept on skating, so effectively and impressively in fact that, when the permanent commissions were announced, he was once again installed as a company commander.

SOME FINAL CAUTIONS

I want to end this chapter with some suggestions that are, in part, encapsulations of what I've written earlier. The first is, *if it feels good, don't.* There are times when telling someone off, walking out of a meeting, or going around someone to that person's boss would prove eminently satisfying. At times, you may have a fiduciary responsibility to do the last of these, for example if a colleague is acting illegally or unethically. But, unless you have such a responsibility, err on the side of restraint.

The second suggestion is closely related to the first: *when in doubt, don't.* As with nearly all proverbs, another exists that communicates the opposite message, *he who hesitates is lost.* When it comes to capitalizing on opportunities, the latter proverb is often applicable; it's similar to, *strike while the iron is hot.* But heed your cautionary instincts, which more often than not will be correct. If it doesn't feel right, stop! Proceed no further.

Third, *don't criticize in front of other people.* Chastising someone in the presence of others, for example during a videoconference, is almost always a bad idea. Follow the adage, *praise in public and criticize in private.* No one likes to be dressed down in front of an audience.

Fourth, as an extension of the above guideline, *don't copy others on messages containing criticism.* This mostly relates to e-mails. It's nearly always better to deliver criticism privately and face to face, and to follow the seven-to-one rule if you possibly can. But, if you must use e-mail to give correctives, copy no one. If and when you critique a subordinate, word will get around. You won't need to broadcast it by including others on the copy line.

Fifth, *don't try to resolve conflicts by e-mail.* I learned this the hard way, and I can tell you that I'll never make that mistake again. It nearly cost me the love of a family member I cherish. When you talk with someone, even on the telephone, each of you can adjust, in real time, everything from intonation to volume, and you can insert quick qualifiers that you simply can't using only the written word. And, if you're talking face to face, both of you also have the benefit of being able, instantaneously, to send nonverbal messages such as a smile.

Finally, *lose control in a controlled manner.* There are occasions when losing your composure can be highly effective for getting a point across, since it's almost certain to get people's attention. Use this kind of shock tactic rarely if at all. Keep in mind that any such apparent loss of control should be grounded in stability. Avoid eruptions and explosions.

THIRTEEN

Nobility: Altruism and Selflessness

Do you demonstrate altruism and selflessness, or do those around you believe you care more about your own outcome than the mission of the enterprise? Are you working for something beyond your next paycheck, bonus, or promotion—a higher purpose? Are you willing, within reason, to subordinate self-interest to the welfare of others? Do they sense that you care about them?

Not long ago, the CEO of a large and well-known conglomerate was fired after only six months. An outside observer might have concluded that underlying his abrupt release was a case of terminal egocentricity. Overriding the authority of the heads of his subsidiaries, he insisted on making a change that would have cost the parent company millions of dollars a year, while hundreds of employees were being laid off—all in the interest of displaying his name more prominently.

It's convenient to conclude that the CEO was simply unwise. No doubt this was so. But, there appears to have been something else going on. What he wanted to do seems to have shown a definite callousness, a striking disconnect between him and the welfare of those employees about to hit the bricks. He appears to have lacked personal nobility, which I suspect ultimately led to his firing. It's likely the board no longer trusted his judgment.

But there are also encouraging stories from corporate America. I once watched a CEO, when he was about to retire, turn down an oil painting hanging in his office. It was worth at least $125,000 at the time and I'm sure has appreciated substantially since then. The corporation offered it to him as a retirement gift, but he declined, in the belief that it would do more good in the corporation where others could continue to enjoy it.

It often becomes obvious who is, and who is not, committed to the long-term health of an enterprise. At least it's obvious to all but those self-absorbed souls who remain oblivious to everything but the size of their next raise or, if they work in a large for-profit company, options grant. Egoistic self-enhancers rarely fare well. This is because they break the rules and don't play fair. These rules are not written down, but just about everyone knows what they are.

In Chapter 12, we referred to the residual rules of society, standards that nearly everyone observes but few of us have ever been explicitly taught. There are similar rules that govern organizational life. If, for example, someone is up against a tight deadline and needs to cut ahead in line, we're expected to allow this. Or, if someone asks for help on a problem and we have the time, we're supposed to provide it. Just as countries or regions have different residual rules—it is not at all ill mannered in certain parts of the world to eat with your fingers—different organizations have different residual rules. Nonetheless, such rules are more alike than different.

Many people consider it bad form to talk about goodness in a business context, perhaps because they don't feel comfortable talking about its opposite, badness. To some, such morally laden terms as *evil* sound grossly outdated, anachronistic. Regardless of what you call it, goodness is critically important to an enterprise. We expect it from one another, and when others don't treat us in the way we expect, we feel diminished. Although the golden rule is, "Do unto others as you would have them do unto you," many people are skilled at modifying this to, "I expect you to treat me as I imagine I would, in my better moments, treat you." There are, in other words, standards of goodness to which they loosely hold themselves but tightly hold others.

Blatant self-promoters skirt the unwritten rules. While some people pay significant personal costs to advance the enterprise, whether it's a publishing company or a food bank, self-serving narcissists are reluctant to pay any cost that fails to bring them individual success and recognition. They advance themselves, without regard to the larger organization, other than treating it as a stage on which to posture and perform. Because they refuse to give at the office when it doesn't directly result in a personal benefit, others eventually figure this out and refuse to give to them. Sooner or later these others say to themselves, "I've got your number," and thenceforth find themselves somehow too busy to assist. Once this happens, the self-promoter is on the path to extinction.

Neither you nor I go to work out of pure altruism. Work is hard, and if we weren't paid to do it, we probably wouldn't, or at least not with the intensity we do. But, there has to be a balance between looking out for ourselves, taking care of other individuals, and looking after the overall organization.

If you go too far in the selfish direction, you'll end up in the organization's arctic zone; if you spend too much of your time taking care of others, you and the enterprise will suffer because your assigned work won't get done; if you work too long and hard for the organization, you'll end up giving so much that you'll burn out, endanger your health, and jeopardize your relationships.

GIVING AND TAKING

As Bill Gates said at a meeting of the World Economic Forum, "there are two great forces of human nature—self-interest and caring for others."[1] He was talking specifically about capitalism vis-à-vis philanthropy, but the same two forces operate within the walls of all organizations. Some people are takers, while others are givers.

Both the *McKinsey Quarterly* and *Harvard Business Review* recently ran articles by Adam Grant, a business professor at Wharton. His subject was giving and taking within organizations, and both pieces were preludes to his book, *Give and Take*. In it, he stresses how important it is for any enterprise to embody a culture of giving, one in which people readily help each other. This, he points out, is at the core of effective collaboration and teamwork. In the *HBR* article, he discusses the need to protect givers from predatory takers, and suggests three traps in which givers may find themselves.

The first is hesitancy, being reluctant to ask for help when it's needed. Second, there's unbounded availability, routinely leaving the door open so others can drop in whenever they like, with the result that the helper doesn't get his or her own work finished. Third, there's the trap of misplaced empathy, overidentification with the person who wants and needs help. Because it's important to strike the right balance between giving and taking in an organization, I want to repeat in modified form his recommendations for how to avoid these traps.

One remedy for reluctance to request help when you need it is to ask on behalf of someone else. Rather than personally asking for assistance, ask on behalf of your team. Or, ask for some group with whose interests yours naturally and truthfully align. Hiding behind someone else like this may not be ideal, but it's sometimes better than having one's own needs continually bypassed in favor of those who find it easier to ask for help.

If you're too available, you leave yourself open to all sorts of random requests, but worse, you cheapen the coin of the realm. I have done this more than once, with the result that I became less productive, wasted a lot of time repeatedly going over the same territory, and subtly encouraged the other person to devalue my help by taking it for granted. The trick here is to limit when you're available. For example, "Before noon, on Wednesdays and Fridays, I'd prefer not to be disturbed." Or, flipping around the paradigm, "I'll be available every day after 2:00." Naturally, we all have to make exceptions. Urgent matters may have to be attended to. But, you should not make such exceptions more often than you have to. Try to schedule specific windows of availability, or if that doesn't suit your flow of work, of unavailability.

Grant is surely right when he warns against "shrewd takers" who manipulatively pull on you for favors. In such cases, he recommends moving from a strategy of empathy to one I think of as discernment. Pause and try to determine what the other person actually needs, which may not be what he or she is asking for. Such discernment is almost always better than reflexively dropping everything to help, which automatically accepts and endorses the other person's analysis of and solution to the problem. The seduction, here, is that it feels good to be needed, something to be especially wary of with certain people.

I have run through these countermeasures because, to avoid the traps, you usually have to be aware of and know how to maneuver around them. Strive for something resembling a fair exchange. The person to whom you give the most may not be the one from whom you receive the most, but at least in rough terms you should get your investment back. You may not get it all back, for the obvious reason that you may have more to give. Just be on guard against those out to extract everything they can without reciprocating.

Grant writes, "when helping is based on a sense of mastery and personal choice rather than duty and obligation, it's more likely to be energizing than exhausting." Helping is indeed more satisfying when it's intentional and voluntary rather than obligatory and coerced.

INTEGRITY

At the end of Chapter 6, there's a brief discussion of the importance of integrity to leadership. I'd like to explore this subject in more detail here. Since we were children, we may have heard that honesty is the best policy. True enough. We may also have heard that if we're honest because honesty is the best policy, our honesty is flawed. Perhaps so. But it is still the best policy.

Without it, society couldn't function because, devoid of honesty, we wouldn't be able to rely on anyone else's word. Commerce would grind to a halt, and we would soon find ourselves foraging in the woods. Being able to depend on promises and the exchange of promises is, in part, what German philosopher Immanuel Kant had in mind when he formulated his *categorical imperative,* one version of which is that we should act as if the rules that govern our actions also governed everyone else's.

The word *integrity,* as we commonly use it, means unwavering adherence to a clear and coherent ethical code. I'd like to suggest that we think of it as the desire to remain beyond reproach in three areas: finances, promises, and assertions. This means to refrain from taking what does not belong to us, do what we say we'll do, and communicate truthfully.

If someone steals *for* your enterprise, that person may also steal *from* it. If you fail to keep your commitments to someone you conclude doesn't matter, you might also fail to keep commitments in general. And, if you say what isn't true, perhaps because doing so is convenient, why should others believe anything you say? Most of us understand why people shouldn't steal. We also know why it's not good to break promises, why we should do what we say we're going to. And, we generally know why it's important not to lie. Because we can lie in subtle ways, however, I want to pay particular attention to veracity—strictly adhering to the truth.

Although many of us wouldn't dream of telling a lie of commission, an overt falsehood, we might, without thinking twice, engage in a lie of omission. If we withhold information, especially of a material nature from someone who could benefit from it, we are already lying. This sometimes occurs out of sheer laziness. Lies of omission can be just as damaging as lies of commission. If people are about to step off a cliff and we don't warn them, our passivity could prove lethal. Treacherous cliffs abound.

But I want to take up an even more subtle kind of lying that Harry G. Frankfurt wrote about in a tiny but powerful book, *On Bullshit.* In it, the Princeton philosopher describes how many people move through life talking authoritatively about things they don't understand. Ask them about anything, and they'll give you an expert opinion. We don't have space here to go into detail about this intriguing topic. My purpose in mentioning it is to warn you against slipping into a pattern of false omniscience because once others detect it, rebuilding your reputation for knowing what you're talking about might prove difficult.

If others conclude you are ethically unsound, they will have difficulty trusting you. Even otherwise good people can become compromised within minutes if they haven't thought through the issues ahead of time. This, in fact, happened to a very fine man who has assisted me in giving workshops on ethics.[2]

After the first of three hours, he silently enters the back of the room and, at my request, tells his story. I watch jaws drop in shocked silence. He shares how an older man he admired, someone who'd been his mentor and sponsor, asked him, a few minutes before the markets closed, to move a large sum of money from one account to another. His purpose was to hide the fact that a publicly traded investment fund he'd founded and still controlled was largely devoid of assets, and the auditors were coming. Because moving funds in the service of defrauding investors is a federal offense, both are now convicted felons. What the younger man experienced demonstrates how quickly an otherwise innocent person can be drawn into trouble. The older fellow was to him a kind of hero, and the young man had no idea, until he was asked to move the money, that the fund was bogus.

At times, people can show surprisingly little ethical courage, a commodity in short supply. This is why it stands out as a special virtue in any organization where the stakes are high. We are quick to think of courage in relation to physical combat, the kind required of law enforcement officers and members of the armed forces. But courage also assumes more subtle forms. These have to do with owning up and taking responsibility for what one either believes or has done—moral fortitude.

I know of one senior leader who, I was later told, backed his car into another one in the company's parking garage and never even left a note. This man was extremely well paid, which made his act of cowardice all the more grievous. It would have been economically trivial for him to own up. Even if it wasn't, leaving a note was the right thing to do. Moreover, not to leave one is a criminal offense. His colleagues apparently referred to him as unethical, but I don't think anyone ever said this to his face. Reputations for honorability can change quickly, sometimes as the result of a single sleazy act, and when they do there is almost nothing that will resuscitate them. And, like this man, you will probably never know.

Some leaders develop reputations for leaving others in the lurch, hanging them out to dry. I've known a few who in meetings would not volunteer that an unpopular idea advanced by a subordinate was, in fact, theirs. They just let the subordinate twist in the wind. What, exactly, is the subordinate to do? Neither taking the fall nor pointing to a boss who wants to remain invisible is an attractive option.

I used to think that the failure to engage in bad behavior was all that was required for a leader to be ethical. That opinion was naïve. Failure to summon the courage to engage in good behavior, especially when such behavior is important, is just as unethical. Is it ethical to refuse to jump into the ocean to save a drowning child because you don't want your suit to get wet?

Nelson Mandela said this about courage and leadership: "It is better to lead from behind and to put others in front, especially when you celebrate victory, when nice things occur. You take the front when there is danger. Then people will appreciate your leadership."[3] Other people will be more likely to trust you if they see you as courageous. If, however, they detect that you are uncourageous, they will *appear* to trust you only as long as it's in their interest to do so. When it's not, they will abandon you.

THE DESIRE TO SERVE

In Chapter 7, we considered the idea of *servant leadership,* an approach to management that was spawned over fifty years ago at A.T.&T. Servant leadership means to ask yourself continually what you can do to make your organization better, and how you can make it more likely for others in it to succeed. Through the years, I've noticed a few people I regard as true servant leaders being put off by this two-word phrase.[4] They believe they sense a certain weakness in the idea of serving, perhaps because it sounds like becoming passive and defaulting on responsibility.

Note how we speak of military, political, and foreign *service,* and of countless other kinds. And, we speak of a person *serving* as an executive. Or, a frontline manager, as in, "We've asked Joan to *serve* as group lead." Although we may not think consciously about the word *service,* we mean just that when we use it in such contexts. As part of everyday life, we're always looking to see if those who attempt to lead us have come to take their positions for granted, asking what they can get, more than what they can give. To borrow the late President Kennedy's paradigm, ask not what your organization can do for you but what you can do for your organization.

No one is always a servant leader, consistently altruistic and perfectly selfless. Nor, perhaps, should anyone be. We've been granted a life, and we have a moral duty to care for that life—from eating wisely and getting enough sleep, to exercising regularly and not burning ourselves out. Among our most fundamental ethical dilemmas is how much to take care of ourselves and how much to take care of others, how much to serve and how much to be served. As suggested earlier, there has to be a balance.

To the extent others see you as putting their needs above or at least on a par with yours, they will be inclined to trust you. No one is drawn to a leader whose first and only concern is self-aggrandizement or wealth accumulation. Talent by itself can only take you so far. What they make of your heart has to get you the rest of the way.

It also helps to show a bit of modesty. Within the context of our highly competitive society, this may seem like an odd recommendation. If, however, you think of its opposite, arrogance, I think you will see why I've made it. Arrogance is often rooted in insecurity. Unlike insecure leaders, confident ones do not spend their time chasing tinsel prizes that add nothing to their substance. Such adornments can be press clippings, honorary board seats, or awards. Nor do they waste their time bragging. A leader *can* be confident and modest at the same time—always a delight. Modest leaders are poised leaders. They know they've been blessed with talents and opportunities. People notice confident modesty as much as insecure arrogance. When they perceive the latter, trust declines.

COMMITMENT AND FOCUS

Those from boardrooms to boiler rooms want to know if their leaders can be trusted to come through. Can they be counted on?

Most successful people show high levels of commitment. They are not always the smartest. But, by and large, they are often the most determined. Successful leaders do what it takes, whatever it takes, within legal and ethical limits. Whether you're leading a charity or directing a museum, running a factory or an arm of government, managing a television studio or a soup kitchen, dedication is a necessary condition if you want to succeed. It's not optional. Fortitude and tenacity count. This, of course, is directly related to what we discussed in Chapter 6.

I've noticed a pattern in many people with high levels of dedication. If they need a specific competence, they will find a way to acquire it. They are clever at figuring out what skills are, and are not, central to what they're doing. If, for example, they need legal help, they are not necessarily going to enroll in law school. They'll consult an attorney. If, however, they need to understand the intricacies of specialized economics for their core businesses, they will devote whatever time they need to master them.

Some people don't have anywhere near this kind of single-minded dedication and often can't seem to get organized enough to keep things moving. Always there are fits and starts, but rarely any consistent follow-through, with the result that they dash about frantically putting out fires. All of this, of course, chews up their time and energy, and because of inefficiency, they get comparatively little done. They'll be motivated for a while on *this* today, but tomorrow it will be *that*.

I'm not arguing against work–life balance, and in my opinion a great many Americans work too much. The average employed American takes about thirteen days of vacation a year, and many work far more than forty hours a week. Compare that with the patterns of certain countries in Europe, where employees complain about working thirty-five hours, and the typical worker gets six weeks of vacation, including the entire month of August. Off to Costa del Sol, Provence, or Majorca. I am, however, arguing for the kind of dedication that causes a person to get a project done with excellence.

Nothing shows how much you care more than taking the initiative. It's not enough to be reactive. The effective leader is proactive, someone who sees where the tribe needs to go and leads them there, often in a way that leaves them feeling like they wanted to go there all along.

I once knew a young banking manager who routinely anticipated his supervisor's needs. If his boss decided one morning that he wanted an analysis of checking accounts, the manager would already have completed one; it was lying in a drawer of his desk. He'd simply wait a day before delivering it. He did this over and over, and almost always overdelivered. If the supervisor wanted a branch analysis appended to a report, he'd already completed one.

Many consultants make a good living by *anticipatory problem solving,* which is what the banking manager was doing. He wasn't only acting before being asked, but continually scanning the environment for opportunities to act, often those no one else had thought of—genuine needs that went unrecognized. Good leaders show these same talents and tendencies. They don't wait for someone else to tell them what to do. They act. And, most of the time, they'd rather ask for forgiveness than permission.

To achieve anything of significance, you almost always have to establish *meaningful* and *measurable* goals. Goals have to be meaningful or you will become bored and tired of them, which is likely to lead to giving up. They also have to be measurable so that you know, at least in general, if you've achieved them. And, you have to pursue them relentlessly. Finally, you should be able, quickly and easily, to explain to anyone *why* these are your goals. In military language, it is always important for others to understand the commander's intent, to be able to answer the question "Why" by completing the phrase "In order to . . ." The mission and its rationale should be clear.

Although this is not a book on organizational planning, I recommending establishing *four to six key goals,* and subordinating everything else in your work–life to them. If you pursue too many goals, all vying for time and energy, your attention may become so diffusely focused that you achieve few of them. The enemies of achievement are complexification and distraction, while its friends are simplification and focus.

Make your goals straightforward enough for a child to understand, since complexity breeds confusion and dilution of purpose. Streamline your calendar so that little or nothing gets in the way of making progress toward your key strategic goals. And, stratify them into primary goals, which are your four to six, and secondary or tertiary ones. Prioritize. First things first.

If you can impose this kind of structure and discipline on yourself, others will be more likely to trust your clear-mindedness and focus, and so be more willing to come along for the ride. If, however, your efforts and energies are splattered all over the landscape, so it's never clear what you're trying to accomplish, others will be uncertain and reluctant to follow. This is not where you want them to be. Nor where you want to be in relation to them.

In Chapter 4, we examined strategic drift, the tendency of a leader or organization to lose sight of objectives. Avoiding drift is a matter of focus. Some leaders skip from objective to objective, never carrying an objective forward from one day to the next. Because of this lack of constancy, they are rarely top performers. Many aspects of leadership require sustained focus and careful attention—everything from planning what you're going to say before picking up the phone, to figuring out to whom to delegate this task or that. Of major importance is staying on course with your objectives, thereby protecting yourself and your organization from strategic drift.

WINSOME GENEROSITY

There are at least three domains in which you can be generous: money, time, and energy. If you come across as miserly in any one of them, others will see it and remember. Naturally, if you're imprudent with how you deploy your tangible or intangible resources, opportunists will find you. Like sharks, they will maneuver you into paying the check. Or, they'll steal your time and sap your energy. You, therefore, have to be wise.

People can be odd about money. Even if they're well off, some will calculate to the penny how much they should leave as a tip at a restaurant, as if this were an exact science, or God declared 17 percent to be the proper amount rather than 15 or 20 percent. Or, at an intimate luncheon, they will compute what each person ordered and should therefore pay, rather than dividing the total bill in a way that seems roughly fair. Such behavior, especially by the affluent, has always impressed me as small-minded.

What if you end up paying for lunch a little more often than you technically should? Does it matter? If and when it starts to feel one-sided, especially if this begins to eat at you, try asking with a puzzled look on your face, "Didn't I pay last time?" If the other person insists you didn't, find a new dining partner.

I've gone into all this to emphasize that it's important to be large-minded when it comes to minor matters like restaurant checks. Why? Because people have invisible recording machines in their heads, and it's not good to develop a reputation for being cheap. Never make the mistake of assuming those who earn or have more money automatically believe they should pay proportionally more. Sharing a meal is not an occasion for progressive taxation. If anything, the financially advantaged are more sensitive than others to being economically exploited. Rightly so.

If someone owes you money and they forget to pay you back, remind them. Always. It's never virtuous to let yourself build up resentment over an unpaid debt. This does no one a favor, especially because the other person may have forgotten. I once lent a company president $100 because he'd forgotten to get cash. That $100 bill was all I had on me, and he was about to leave for the airport. Several weeks went by without repayment, so I reminded him. As I suspected, he'd simply forgotten.

When it comes to managing your time, you have to be wise. Time management is in reality task management, since we all have the same number of hours in a week. And, task management ultimately comes down to prioritization, intuitively sensing how much time to devote to what tasks—and to which people. If there's anything effective leaders do well, it's prioritize, which means they carefully manage their time. They rarely let anyone waste it. But, being a good steward of time doesn't mean being stingy with it. Helping other people, and doing so from the heart, is indeed noble, and sometimes a gift others long remember.

By all means, go ahead and demonstrate this virtue, as long as you believe the person you're helping is profiting from your assistance. If and when they aren't, make yourself less available. You have to distinguish between slow learners—those who may be otherwise gifted but have little feel for administration or management—and those who mostly want to consume your time by embroiling you in empty chatter, with no desire to change. Or, who play, *Yes, but.* These are the ones who have endless excuses for why they've yet to follow your advice.

Of the three—money, time, and energy—the last is the most challenging to regulate. This is because all expenditures of energy are not equal. You can spend an hour with one person and find yourself invigorated. That same hour spent with someone else might leave you drained. Give in abundance to those you find nourishing, but more cautiously to those you don't.

KNIGHTS AND VASSALS

Some leaders are admirably altruistic, while others are blatantly self-centered. Still others care more about ensuring that the stock price is high when they retire than about the long-term worth of the company they're supposed to be leading.[5] We all want to work for an enterprise run by leaders who care more about *it* and its mission than how much money they make, or how they look in the *Wall Street Journal* or even an association newsletter. Your subordinates, as well as your peers, will want to support you to the degree that they recognize in you the sort of nobility we tend to associate with mediaeval knights.

If you think of an organization as comprised of knights and vassals, those below you in the hierarchy want to believe in you, their knight and champion, just as you want to believe in the nobles above you. Subordinates will trust you only if they regard you as worthy. They inwardly long to perceive you as working for something larger than yourself or your portfolio. They want to see you as striving for the greater good, a grander purpose. Many desperately need to believe you to be working for *them* as well as *you,* and more broadly for *society.*

Be their worthy champion.

FOURTEEN

Compassion: Sympathetic Concern and Empathic Understanding

How well do you understand and care about what others are going through, whether inside the organization or in their personal lives? Can you accurately read what they think and feel? Do you empathize with them in their struggles, and effectively communicate that empathy? Or, to the contrary, when someone encounters a problem or shares a setback, do you rush past their experience, perhaps on the way to offering only platitudes or superficial advice? Is it clear to others that you desire, when and where you can, to help them?

This is a chapter that many readers might be tempted to skip. I imagine these kinds of thoughts running through their minds: I manage an organization, which means getting results, and I don't have time for maudlin sentimentality. There's the budget, revenues, expenses, and most of all time-urgent deliverables. None of this has *anything* to do with compassion.

If you entertain such thoughts, do not skip this chapter. Appropriate compassion may have a lot more to do with productivity than you think, and by implication a lot more to do with effective leadership. Here is one dictionary definition of compassion: "Deep awareness of the suffering of another coupled with the wish to relieve it."[1]

Compassion requires human sensitivity, the capacity and inclination to respond to others and what they are communicating, verbally or nonverbally. The term *sensitivity* has at least two meanings. If, for example, we say, "Pat is sensitive," we may mean Pat is touchy, over-reactive, and makes mountains out of molehills. Or, on the contrary, we may mean Pat is a caring person who's in close touch with how other people experience life. It is only in this second sense that I'm using it. Such sensitivity is necessary for both empathy and sympathy, which together serve as the foundations for compassion.

EMPATHY, SYMPATHY, AND COMPASSION

Empathy is tuning in to what others are experiencing. The first definition of empathy that appears in the same dictionary is, "Identification with and understanding of another's situation, feelings, and motives."[2] This is a particularly fine definition in that it highlights the importance of identification. Empathy involves temporarily accepting others' frames of reference, seeing the world through their eyes, and adopting their points of view. If you're a highly empathic person, you may even feel in your body something resembling what the other person physically experiences. Their anxiety becomes yours; their stomach pains become your stomach pangs.

This kind of mirroring is the basis for emotional contagion. You may catch the discomfort of other people simply by being around them when they're distressed. Perhaps you've had the experience of spending time with someone who was anxious or depressed, and discovering that you began to feel the same way. And, you may also catch their happiness and joy.

You can even observe emotional contagion in babies. When one infant begins to cry, others may start to cry also. Contagion, as used here, is a metaphor. There is no physical pathogen involved, and precisely why adults or babies seem to catch each other's psychological states remains unclear. When it comes to babies beginning to cry when others do, the proximate cause may simply be the loud noise of other infants crying, but primitive identification also probably plays a role.

Perhaps the most helpful dictionary definition for sympathy is this one: "A feeling or an expression of pity or sorrow for the distress of another."[3] Sympathy is recognizing that others are suffering. It is not so much characterized by identifying and connecting, as by feeling sorry for them. Figure 14.1 depicts how empathy and sympathy sometimes combine to impel a person to take compassionate action, to do something to alleviate the suffering. You usually have to feel sorry for *and* identify with others to take action on their behalf.

You can feel sympathy, even pity, for others without understanding much of what they're going through; if you can't understand how they feel,

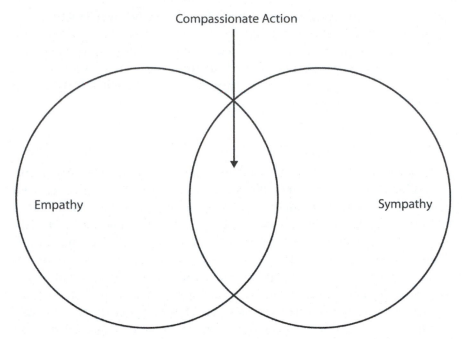

Figure 14.1

you can't empathize. And, if you can't empathize, you'll be less likely to do something to help. Unless sympathy is accompanied by empathy, there is little human-to-human linking, so the relationship is characterized by what Martin Buber called "I-It" rather than "I-Thou."[4]

You can also empathize without finding yourself particularly sympathetic, so again you may not be inclined to take action. We will consider an example of how this could be the case further on in this chapter.

EXTREMES ON THE CONTINUUM OF COMPASSION

When some people watch a realistic film of a person being tortured, maimed, or killed, they find it profoundly disturbing and quickly turn away. Their hearts pound, their blood pressures rise, and adrenalin courses through their bloodstreams. They sweat, feel queasy, and become ill. Such a film proves so distressing that they have flashbacks of it for days or even months.

Other people, watching the same film, are not at all moved. It's not *their* bodies, their lives that are being affected. They may regard what is happening as unfortunate and even sad, but they experience little or no personal identification with the victim. He or she remains more an object, a thing, than a fellow human being.

These two groups differ markedly and fall at opposite ends of a continuum. Those in the first group overidentify with the one who suffers, and such overidentification becomes incapacitating; those in the second group remain detached. Overidentifying with a suffering human being is never going to be their problem. They are far more likely to underidentify. Others may describe them as unfeeling, lacking in warmth, and devoid of compassion.

Not long ago, I asked a senior manager to name who, among the executives we both knew, impressed him as the most compassionate. I did this, in part, to see how well our perceptions matched. The first name he came up with was the same one I had in mind, a former CEO who was strong but gentle, clear-minded but open, and most of all humanely sensitive. He was, and is, the consummate gentleman, and without putting on airs, quietly aristocratic. You instinctively know he understands what life is like for *you* and that he cares.

I once watched him convene a meeting, in the ballroom of a hotel, for 300 employees who worked for his company. He had just been promoted to run it, and drastic measures had to be taken. When he took the podium, he welcomed everyone and then told them that, at the end of the month, over 90 percent of them wouldn't be there. When he brought the meeting to a close, they actually applauded. This was, I believe, because they knew he had compassion for them, as individuals and as a group—as human beings.

COMPASSION AND CONNECTING

Leadership, as we have seen, hinges on getting others to trust and connect with you. This is difficult if not impossible to achieve if you remain detached and disconnected. Those you desire to lead have to sense that, in some fundamental way, you understand how they see the world and what life is like for them day by day. All good leaders form a strong but invisible bond with their followers. In just about any organization, interpersonal sensitivity functions like glue, cementing the relationship between leaders and followers. Even if you run an organization of thousands, most of whom will never speak with you personally, it is important to communicate that you know what it feels like in the trenches. The more they see that you understand what they're going through, the more loyal they will be. Empathy is an immensely valuable commodity, whether in a small business, a government agency, a nongovernmental organization, a charity, or a conglomerate.

Compassion requires at least these qualities:

1. Awareness of your own psychological processes, the sort of insight into your inner workings discussed in Chapter 11. Of cardinal importance is that you are acutely conscious of how you think and feel, how this affects what you do, and why.

2. The willingness to pay attention to what others reveal to you about *their* inner workings. You have to listen and show you're interested.

3. An ability to read the true nature of the other person's experience, to tell the difference, for example, between contented happiness and overwhelming joy, between feeling down and deep depression. Some people have little difficulty putting their feelings into words, while others, even if highly intelligent, find this task challenging. You have to be able to fathom what they can't or don't verbalize, to pick up on nonverbal cues.

4. Seeing the links between what they're experiencing and what you may have gone through. These links have to be genuine and meaningful. Someone permanently in a wheelchair does not want to hear about how you broke your arm when you were twelve. When I was a professor, one of the doctoral students, years earlier as a teenager, dove off a cliff into a river, hit his head on a rock, and ended up paralyzed. For several years, I had him come into my class in psychotherapy and tell his fellow students what disabled people do, and do not, want to hear. He shared how he'd had the experience of another person, in a well-meaning but misguided attempt to empathize, telling him about once having broken a toe.

5. Fluency at communicating *what* you understand and that you care. You have to be able to put into words an accurate grasp of how the other person feels. Most of all, you have to avoid resorting to cold, insensitive, and insulting clichés, such as, "It sounds like you're bipolar" or "You may suffer from OCD."

6. A strong desire to do what you can to ameliorate whatever suffering they might be going through.

One manager I know is very good to subordinates, from ensuring that they are well compensated, to speaking up for them in succession planning meetings. But something important is missing: awareness of how much better performance he could get from them by demonstrating more human sensitivity. Although he is admired for his competence, subordinates privately speak of him as cold and aloof. As a result, they do not work up to their full capacity, and he ends up doing their jobs for them.

I also know a senior executive whose organization runs exceptionally well, and has for many years. Yet, he never seems to strain. Somehow, the railroads run on time, as if by magic. Only it isn't magic. It's world-class leadership. Undergirding this leadership is the empathic bond he's created with his direct reports, who are fiercely loyal and would rather face a firing squad than disappoint him. He, in turn, is loyal to them and more inclined to inspire than punish. This man cares about them, and they know it. As I suggest elsewhere in this book, great art is to make it look effortless, and he does. The beauty of this seemingly effortless magic is that he never makes anyone miserable. He enjoys warm relationships with everyone who's ever worked for him.

In Chapter 5, we noted that, regardless of their relative ages, leaders stand *in loco parentis* to those they lead—they function as quasi-parents whose encouragement and approval are valued. If you want to get the most out of your subordinates, you have to encourage and occasionally push them, but you also have to function like a nourishing rather than critical parent. Nourishing parents empathize with, have sympathy for, and show compassion toward their kids.

CHARACTERISTICS OF COMPASSIONATE PEOPLE

People with a high capacity for compassion can usually read what others find motivating. For some, it's a pat on the back and a private "well done." For others, it's showing interest in their families, perhaps their children. Or, public recognition. Maybe for others, it's taking them to lunch. And for still others, it's talking with them about the organization. They simply want to know what's going on.

Highly in-touch people quickly sense when others want to be included and, whenever possible, make efforts to include them. In a conversation, they intuitively understand what the other person wants to talk about and tend to adjust the dialogue accordingly. When they're addressing an audience, if what they're saying or how they're saying it requires redirection or modification, they smoothly make adjustments (see Chapter 11). Interpersonally sensitive people also know when to stop talking. They don't go on and on, oblivious to how off-putting monologues can be, and how others may be thinking, *Come up for air!*

Truly compassionate individuals are rarely if ever told they're insensitive. They are empathic and therefore able to zero in on how others feel, appreciate *why* they feel as they do, and anticipate their reactions. Compassionate people sense when someone is comfortable or uncomfortable, and they tend to attract other people, who instinctively know they'll be understood. Those who are highly empathic can often intuit the other person's intentions, goals, moods, feelings, values, attitudes, and beliefs.

Like good detectives, interpersonally sensitive people also know when superficial politeness masks deeper hostility, antipathy, or animosity. Statements and questions can be so nuanced that this is not always obvious. Yet, such people seem generally to know when others are sincere or insincere, and by implication whether to believe what they're saying.

HOW COMPASSION WORKS

Here's how the complicated process of compassion works: First, there's taking in data from the other person, turning it into information, and trying to interpret what it signifies—you *infer* what it says about the other person's mental state. Second, there's a quick search-and-retrieve look into yourself, in an attempt to find patterns or templates from your own life that, at least roughly, match your interpretation; all the while, you're trying to *imagine* what the other person is experiencing, and as you do this, you may engage in still more search-and-retrieve. Third, you automatically determine if you can *identify* with the other person.

Compassion, then, involves these three processes: *inference, imagination,* and *identification.* It hinges on attending to what the other person is saying and doing, and recognizing its significance; matching this to your databank of experience, images and sensations from memory; and, finally, seeing yourself in that person.

When we spend time with people, we can't help but notice, at least at a gross level, what they say and how they act. We may or may not pay attention to their clothes or shoes, but we will usually notice the expressions on their faces. We'll also notice and remember what they say, especially if it has a lot of impact on us. Without thinking about it, we register whatever seems out of the ordinary, whether in their words, on their faces, or how they walk. And, based on what we register, we automatically draw conclusions about their inner states.

Drawing such conclusions rests on a certain kind of logic. It's not deductive logic, not like concluding that Socrates is mortal from knowing that all men are mortal and Socrates is a man. That sort of logic is airtight: if it is certain that all men are mortal and Socrates is a man, it is also certain that Socrates is mortal. The logic of compassion, by contrast, is inductive. It has to do, therefore, with probabilities rather than certainties.

Suppose, on the basis of past experience, you know that someone who is crying will often claim to be sad or depressed. You walk down the hall and notice someone crying. It's likely you'll conclude—draw the inference—that the person is sad or depressed. But, you may be wrong. Perhaps he or she is simply having trouble with a contact lens or suffering from an eye infection.

Compassion also relies on imagination, the ability to visualize what it must be like for others to experience what they do, whether having a child, winning the lottery, or losing a job. The inferences you've already drawn will determine what you imagine them to be experiencing, and perhaps also enable you to retrieve what you felt when you went through something similar.

Using your imagination to get inside another person's head and heart typically leads to identification. You come to see yourself as similar to the other person, and also come to regard that person as like you. If, as a leader, you're able effectively to *communicate* human sensitivity to those you lead, they will identify with you. You become *just like them.*

Identification does not imply losing your sense of self or the boundaries between you and another person. It is neither wise nor healthy to blur these boundaries because doing so can cause you to become emotionally overwhelmed. Those who work in critical care professions, such as emergency room physicians and intensive care unit (ICU) nurses, are forever in danger of succumbing to empathic burnout, which is why they have to be especially careful about boundaries.

THE FUTILITY OF UNEXPRESSED COMPASSION

You can have a great deal of empathy and compassion without the ability to express it. All the empathy in the world comes to little or nothing if the other person is unaware of it. When I was a practicing clinician, I saw many couples for marital therapy. Sometimes, they demonstrated a striking lack of compassionate communication. Here are the sorts of complaints I would hear: "He never says he loves me unless we're in bed." Or, "She always reminds me that I haven't finished cleaning the garage, but never says she knows how hard I work." Or perhaps, "I always take care of the kids, hold down a full-time job, and never complain about doing the housework—with never a word of appreciation."[5]

Here's how noncompassionately, and also in the last case defensively, the spouse would sometimes respond to each complaint: To the first, the husband might fire back, "If I didn't love you, I wouldn't be here." To the second, the wife might snap, "That's ridiculous! Of course I know how hard you work." And to the third, the husband might reply, "I'm doing just as much as you are!" Compassion is a kind of food, and without it people starve.

THE IMPORTANCE OF ACCURACY

Some people are quick to say they understand when they don't. If you try to show compassion toward someone but are on the wrong track, it can prove worse than not trying to do so in the first place. We may project our own characteristics onto another person, and then identify with that person solely because of such projected (imagined) characteristics.

Here's an example of how this can work: Julia tells Sally that Julia's father just passed away. Sally recalls how much she loved her own father, whose death triggered in her a long period of reactive depression. So she says, "I know exactly what you're going through. It's a terrible loss when a father dies. I can see how devastated you are." Sally, however, doesn't realize that Julia and her father were estranged since she was nine, that he was an abusive alcoholic who contributed neither alimony nor child support to Julia's mother, and that Julia was relieved rather than depressed when her father died. Julia is certainly not devastated. She no longer has to worry about him showing up intoxicated on her doorstep. To tell someone your story and get back nothing but irrelevancies is like saying you're thirsty and having someone bring you a box of cereal.

LISTENING AND VERIFYING

To perceive what another person is communicating accurately, you have to listen, which means enduring some awkward silence now and then. Doing this is not easy, because silence tends to generate anxiety; we may feel like we're not helping if we say nothing, especially when the other person isn't talking. But you'll never appreciate what you can learn during such silences if you automatically fill them in with awkward chatter. Sometimes, the most helpful thing you can do is simply *be there*. No advice. No platitudes. No stories about you. Just your presence.

When, not having rushed in to fill the silence, you believe you've grasped what the other person is expressing, you can test the accuracy of your empathy. "Let me see if I understand" is a good way to lead into trying to capture in words what you've heard. Or, "It sounds like . . . am I right?" Or simply, "I'd like to say it back, to make sure I have it."

DYSFUNCTIONS OF THE HEART

If you were to ask a psychologist or psychiatrist to give you a one-sentence definition of a *sociopath,* you might hear something like this: "Someone with a seriously defective conscience." But there's another definition, one that is also piercingly accurate: complete lack of empathy and therefore of compassion. Sociopaths cannot, or at least do not, identify with their victims, who to them are objects. Such emotions as they show are shallow and, more often than not, manipulative. Recall how the two groups of people mentioned at the beginning of this chapter respond to viewing a brutal film. Those in the first group become profoundly distressed, while those in the second remain unmoved. Although not everyone in the second group is sociopathic, a true sociopath might actually enjoy watching such a film.

Another form of psychological dysfunction associated with deficient compassion is *narcissism,* the tendency to be preoccupied with yourself to the exclusion of others and their needs, and to act as if the entire world revolves around you. Self-centered people have a hard time showing empathy. This is because a basic characteristic of all relationships is focus-on-self versus focus-on-other. Whenever you spend time with another person, whether face to face or on the phone, you continually make the choice of whether to focus your attention on the other person or yourself. Asking someone what he or she thinks or feels is focus-on-other, while expressing how you feel is focus-on-self. For narcissists, it's routinely the latter.

A third form of dysfunction is *detachment.* Detached people live in their own worlds and care little about those around them. Their relationships, to the extent they have any, reflect interpersonal distance. Compassion, therefore, is strangely absent.

Finally, there's *cross-cultural insensitivity.* Show me someone with little or no cross-cultural or cross-gender sensitivity, and I'll show you someone with an undersized heart. Research has demonstrated a positive correlation, for example, between racism and misanthropy—hatred of humankind. Racists and other bigots generally mistrust other human beings and, by and large, have little compassion or affection for them.

LIMITS TO COMPASSION

When you're in a position of leadership, you can't always alleviate someone's pain, regardless of how much you empathize—not and perform your job honorably. Compassion does *not* mean putting up with poor performance. Although you may feel sympathy toward and greatly empathize with someone you're about to fire, you may empathize even more with others who've had to pick up the slack, and would in all probability have to do so again if you did not follow through with the termination.

As noted in Chapter 5, I've often advised leaders to avoid turning themselves into amateur psychologists, since doing so invariably puts them in a dual-role relationship. The problem with such relationships is that they bring with them competing sets of duties, and thus create a conflict of interest that can compromise objectivity and cloud judgment. Out of a desire to help, leaders can end up torn between doing their jobs and becoming ad hoc mental health counselors.

INCREASING YOUR CAPACITY FOR COMPASSION

The majority of people, when asked, will say they are above average in interpersonal sensitivity. But, most people also claim to be a better-than-average driver. Both of these claims are mathematically impossible. By definition, only half of us can be above average. It turns out that there is no correlation between self-rated and genuine empathy and, by implication, compassion.[6] I mention this to discourage you from dismissing what follows, in the belief that none of it could benefit you.

Empathy and the compassion it undergirds are sophisticated skills that, for many people, develop throughout life. Many forty-year-olds are more empathic, sympathetic, and compassionate than they were at twenty. This, of course, is good news, since it suggests that people are not born with a fixed amount of, or capacity for, human sensitivity. With effort and attention, empathy and perhaps sympathy also can be cultivated. Here are a few things to do if you want to increase yours:

1. *Remember personal details.* A manager I know in one company asks his subordinates the same questions over and over. Each time, he seems to have forgotten that he's asked the question before and what the answer was. You might think that inquiring about one's wife or aging father would build rapport, contribute to trust, and enhance leadership, but perfunctory questioning and subsequent forgetfulness has the opposite effect. He is resented for what they perceive as going through the motions. "If he really cared, he'd remember what I told him the last three times." Tactfully asking personal questions can be an effective trust builder, but only if you do this sincerely and care enough to remember what questions you've already asked and what the answers were. So many demands may be coming at you that you have trouble

remembering the details. If so, consider keeping a notebook in your desk and jotting them down.

2. *Practice reflective listening.* Reflective listening also goes by the name of active listening. It's saying back to the other person the emotional essence of what you've heard. This does not mean parroting, repeating the same words, which can quickly wear thin. It means truly listening, so that what you say deepens the other person's experience of feeling understood. Learning to do this well takes time, but if you want to connect with people, this is among the best ways to do it.

3. *Verbalize your feelings.* By doing this throughout the day, you will probably increase your emotional fluency, your ability to put moods and feelings into words. I am not naïve about how little time you may have for this, and I realize that such an activity can easily be crowded out by everything else you have to do. But I am confident that if you mentally verbalize what you're feeling as often as you can, you will have a larger empathic vocabulary, a wider range of things to say to others about their feelings when the need arises. When you walk down the hall, ask yourself what you're thinking, and more importantly, what you're feeling.

4. *Read novels.* You probably read more nonfiction than fiction, but reading good novels has the potential to make you more aware of emotional and interpersonal nuances. This is because they encourage and enable you to see events from another person's point of view, whether the story's written in the first person (I) or the third (he and she). Watching movies, however otherwise rewarding (see #5), is not quite the same because they don't give you as much time to reflect on what the characters are thinking, feeling, and doing—and why. If nothing else, take a good novel[7] or two along with you on vacation.

5. *Reduce your stress.* You'll be more compassionate if you are less stressed. Because so much information about stress reduction is available, I won't belabor the subject here, except to suggest that chemicals, such as alcohol or tranquilizers, are not the best long-term options for stress reduction. Better options include regular exercise, breath work, yoga, Tai Chi, lying in a warm bath, getting a massage, or going to a movie, which within ten minutes can put you in a light trance and give you at least a temporary respite from your everyday obligations. Although films can't compete with novels for broadening your perspectives, well-chosen ones can at least help you take stress-reducing breaks.

6. *Ask for feedback about your interpersonal sensitivity.* This is not easy to do, and the higher you rise in any organization, the more difficult it can become. But it is important to recruit a small cadre of people you trust, and who are bold enough to tell you the truth. The key question to ask, of course, is how well you seem to empathize with and show compassion toward other people. Their answers will probably reveal how well they believe you empathize with and show compassion toward *them.* Even friends and allies may be reluctant to tell you the truth, so you have to convince them that you genuinely want to hear what they have to say. It's usually best to seek feedback about your interpersonal sensitivity from trustworthy peers. You and your subordinates have a consequential relationship, which makes the stakes higher for them and in turn can discourage candor. And, your supervisors may shy away from candor because they may be concerned about potentially demoralizing you.

CONCLUDING THOUGHTS

You'll inspire trust, and increase your effectiveness as a leader, to the extent that you care enough to empathize with others and communicate compassion. It's easy to dismiss compassion as a trivial feature on the landscape of leadership, a kind of nice-to-have but not something for which you have a lot of time. If you're as busy as I imagine you to be, it may be difficult to demonstrate much sensitivity. There's so much to accomplish and there's always the trade-off between task and relationship. And, I see nothing to suggest that the task demands on either of us are going to decrease. So, I empathize with your less-than-perfect empathy—and I trust that you, in turn, empathize with mine.

Never underestimate the power of compassion. When you communicate understanding, concern, and a willingness to help, especially to those having a rough time, they are unlikely to forget this. As an example of how memorable a single act of compassion can be, I know a manager whose house, many years ago, unexpectedly went up in flames. With no duty to do so, his corporation gave him a considerable sum of money to help with temporary housing, an act of compassion if ever I saw one. He still speaks of that corporation with appreciation, gratitude, and unbridled affection. If people have long memories for who shows up at weddings and funerals, they have even longer ones for those who understand and reach out to them when they're in trouble or in need.

Compassion is potent medicine. Do not neglect or ignore it.

FIFTEEN

Persuasiveness: Pathways to Social Power and Influence

Can you recruit others to your cause? Are you able to get things done through other people? Can you build teams, motivate subordinates, and convince colleagues to help you, especially when there's nothing in it for them? Do those around you experience you as inspiring, so that they develop a natural predilection to follow you? Can you enroll and enfranchise through persuasion? Do you understand the nature of great leadership?

This chapter brings together much of what we've discussed throughout Part II of this book. Having the social skill to persuade others to do what you want them to do depends on demonstrating the interpersonal attributes we've examined in the last four chapters:

- Knowing yourself and your impact
- Exercising restraint when you feel inclined to lash out
- Making it clear you're interested in the greater good
- Being able to demonstrate compassion.

It's also important, of course, to exemplify the source traits of the Big Five that we reviewed in Part I. Here, for review, is a brief description of each one:

- Strong analytic ability, conceptual thinking, and intuitive reasoning
- Emotional maturity and self-containment

- Goal-directedness and a desire to achieve results
- The capacity to establish and maintain collaborative relationships
- Flexibility when it comes to leading versus following.

Work enables us to be creative but it also involves a certain amount of suffering. Relatively few people would subject themselves to this if they weren't somehow persuaded to. Rewards such as raises, bonuses, and promotions are all vehicles of persuasion. So are adverse consequences, for example negative appraisals, performance improvement plans, and the withholding of rewards. Yet, the most powerful inducement to work diligently over a sustained period is a persuasive leader. Tangible payoffs may often be a necessary condition, but they are rarely a sufficient one for people to show a prolonged willingness to sacrifice for the good of the enterprise.

Leadership is the ability to induce followership. The legendary coach of the Dallas Cowboys, Tom Landry, put it this way: "Leadership is getting someone to do what they don't want to do, to achieve what they want to achieve."

CLARITY ABOUT VISION AND MISSION

Throughout this book, we've seen how important it is for a leader to be clear about his or her overarching purpose and be able to communicate this purpose in a way that can quickly be grasped by supervisors, peers, and most of all subordinates. We also noted in Chapters 4 and 14 that, as a corollary, it's imperative to avoid strategic drift—becoming distracted and, as a consequence, veering off course. Here are the three fundamental components of purpose as it is ordinarily expressed in corporate life: vision, mission, and goals. Because there's confusion about what each one signifies, such that it is common for mission statements to read more like vision statements, and vice versa, I want to clarify the meanings of all three.

A vision is a mental picture of what an organization aspires to *be* in the future, while a mission is what it must *do* to get there. *Vision statements,* as such, do not specify or imply particular actions. Rather, they reduce mental images to writing and, in the ideal, serve as inspiring word-pictures. These captured aspirations are not unrealistic fantasies but future states that are both potentially attainable and a healthy stretch.

Mission statements, to the contrary, specify at the most general or abstract level what must be done to turn visions into realities. Good mission statements are clear, understandable, and brief. They guide concrete decision making throughout the organization, especially when faced with choices that entail trade-offs, which many decisions do.

Good leaders have vision and are able to communicate it quickly and persuasively. They also know and can make crystal clear what needs to be done, at the most general level, to turn that vision into a reality—they know and can articulate the organization's mission.

POWERFUL STRATEGIC GOALS

Strong leaders have well-thought-out goals and can communicate them in a way that persuades others to make them their own. Strategic goals are those small number of primary objectives that must be pursued to carry out the mission and, so, realize the vision. For the sake of this discussion, I am using the term *goal* and *objective* interchangeably. There should be only four to six strategic goals, and if you end up with more, your vision or mission may need sharpening. Such goals should be achievable in two to three years and, as noted in Chapter 13, they should also be both *meaningful* and *measurable.*

You can use a structured process to develop your vision, mission, and goals, perhaps in collaboration with members of your organization, but you cannot fulfill your potential as a leader without getting clear about all three, and making sure your subordinates are also clear. As Rosalynn Carter said, "A great leader takes people where they don't necessarily want to go, but ought to be."

Here are some examples of poor strategic goals, and why I call them that:

"Become more proactive in educating others." About what? How will you measure your proactivity "then" as compared to "now"? By when will you do this?

"Update our technology." Fine, but what technology, by when, and by how much?

"Maintain or increase our financial integrity." Great, but what exactly is this? And, how do you—will you—measure financial integrity. By when do you intend to accomplish this? What are the concrete indices of success?

By contrast, here are some examples of better strategic goals:

"Establish numerical productivity-improvement targets by March 31 of this year, and reach them by January 1 of the year after next."

"By December 31 of this year, develop a mid-term capital project planning process that demonstrably improves project forecasting and conservation of capital."

"By June 1 of next year, publish a finished report that presents simplified job titles and descriptions, families of jobs, and required qualifications for each of these job families."

Many published vision and mission statements are, in reality, collections of strategic goals, perhaps with strategies and tactics thrown in. They fall in the middle level of abstraction. This does not mean that they are without value, and in many cases they help an enterprise considerably. But it does mean they are mislabeled.

STRATEGIES AND TACTICS

It's also important to work out strategies and tactics, and to communicate these also. Here's an example of the difference between a strategy and a set of supporting tactics. Suppose, for the sake of illustration, the city of Portland decided that one fine summer day it was no longer part of the United States, or for that matter, the state of Oregon. Its citizens refuse to pay federal, state, or local taxes, or ever again to file tax forms. Portland declares itself a sovereign country and elects a president. As we know from the Civil War, secession would trigger a swift response. The U.S. government would decide to put an end to this quickly. Retaking the city would become its key objective, its strategic goal.

But, how should this be done? We could send in the Marines followed by an occupying army, but Portland has announced its intention to "fight to the last man." Clearly, boots on the ground as an initial strategy would cost unnecessary lives. We could also disable its access to all information outside of Portland, all means and modes of electronic communication, including the Internet and telephone systems, in the hope that, if the good people of Portland became sufficiently starved for information, they would surrender. But, such surrender would be uncertain. So, let's assume we decided to lay siege to the city, in hopes that this would do the trick. Siege now becomes our strategy.

To accomplish such a siege, we'd have to develop tactics. We might decide to cut off all truck and rail transportation into and out of Portland, to blockade the roads and tear up sections of train track. No more food is going to enter it. We might cut off all electricity flowing into Portland, which would make it impossible to turn on most computers, televisions, and air conditioners. We might also stop the flow of natural gas into the city, so that in addition to nonfunctioning electric stoves, no gas ranges will operate either. These, then, would be the tactics.

EXISTING AND ASPIRATIONAL VALUES

Another mistake, similar to becoming muddled about the difference between vision and mission, is to confuse existing values with aspirational ones. In their classic *Built to Last,*[1] Collins and Porras suggest that every good enterprise has a core ideology, consisting of a core purpose and a set of core values. These values are what they call *essential tenets,* and they are discovered rather than proclaimed. Collins and Porras give this advice: "To identify the core values of your own organization, push with relentless honesty to define what values are truly central." If you end up with more than a few of them, you have to ask if all of them are core, if you might not be confusing core values with something else, such as operating practices or business strategies.

I have seen companies bypass the hard work of determining existing values en route to crafting aspirational ones. There is certainly a place for stating the values to which a company aspires. But it is also important to know the difference between what an enterprise *is* and what it *hopes* to become. If nothing else, this allows you to take a hard look at the gap between the two, and to come up with ways to close that gap.

WISE EMPOWERMENT

Persuasive leaders get things done through other people, and this has a great deal to do with empowerment. But, the level of empowerment is not set in stone. How much you empower another person can change from day to day or even moment to moment, depending on the individual's track record. If someone you've empowered botches an assignment, you are likely to restrict that person's freedom of decision making. If, however, they deliver what you've asked, you will expand this freedom. The following diagram (Figure 15.1) shows how empowerment works. It also reflects how decisions get made, which in the end is what empowerment is about anyway. Notice how, at the bottom of the diagram, empowerment is represented on a continuous scale. It is *not* depicted as simply low or high.

Empowerment is not a static entity but, rather, a dynamic arrangement. It must be negotiated and renegotiated, and it's directly contingent on how much your judgment is trusted. Empowerment, therefore, rests on staying in synch with the wishes and predilections of the person or persons to whom you report. The same reasoning applies to those who report to you—if they want you to empower them, they have to be in synch.

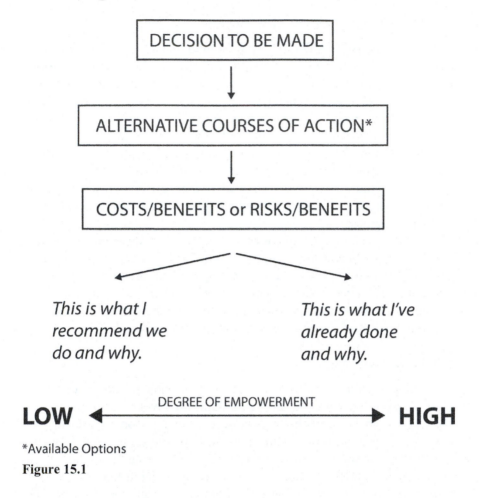

*Available Options
Figure 15.1

Brigadier General Jack Hagan pointed out to me that the midpoint be-
tween the two extremes of empowerment might be captured in the phrase,
"This is what I *intend* to do." The bottom left in the diagram ("This is what
I recommend and why") corresponds to perceiving the leader as saying,
"Don't do anything unless you're told," while the bottom right ("This is
what I've done and why") corresponds to the leader saying, "Just do it."

Here's where the nuanced art of top-flight leadership comes in: If you
trust people, they will tend also to trust you and prove themselves trustworthy. The goal is to empower them, but only to the level at which they'll
succeed; you can slowly increase this level of empowerment. If you give
them more power than they can responsibly and effectively handle, you

set them up for failure. This, of course, means that you also set yourself up for failure. The idea is to bring them along, and stay in close enough touch with what they're doing, or not doing, that you pretty much guarantee their success.

Can you do this with everyone? Of course not. But you may be able to *coach up* more people than you think.

I want to highlight some of the other qualities that make it more likely for a leader to be persuasive. Not all great leaders show all these qualities. But they show most of them. Along the way, we'll note a number of concrete steps you can take to enhance your persuasiveness.

COMPETENCE AND CONFIDENCE

Because competence is one of the two axes of trust around which this book has been organized, I want to repeat that to lead you have to know what you're doing. If you don't, this will eventually become apparent. Never fake it.

If you need advice or assistance to do some part of your job, get it, instead of trying to bluff your way through. There's nothing wrong with relying on the expertise of others, as long as you make a diligent effort to get up to speed. All top-tier leaders both ask for assistance and strive to master whatever content is directly relevant to their job performance. As noted earlier, it's important to lead by the authority of competence rather than the authority of position. Position power, by itself, does not enroll and enfranchise.

It is also important for a leader to act confidently and not vacillate. Asking for feedback in a systematic way is desirable. Constantly checking, in the hope that others will reassure you, isn't. There will be times when you don't know what to do. If you have the luxury of gathering more information, do it. But if you don't, make a decision and stick to it. Even if you're terrified, don't show it because if you communicate uncertainty and equivocation, those around you will trust neither you nor your decisions.

A decision may turn out to be wrong. If so, revise it with the same confidence you demonstrated the first time. Good leaders have a short memory for failure. Leaders should rarely if ever appear unsure, pessimistic, or tired. You have to demonstrate both *tough poise*—resilience—and *efficiency of decision making,* the ability to make decisions with incomplete and imperfect information, which is usually the only kind available anyway.

GOOD AND BAD AMBITION

Many people never become leaders because they are simply not motivated to lead—to persuade. They lack sufficient ambition. Ambition is a word that can be used in at least two senses, one noble and the other base. In Shakespeare's *Julius Caesar,* the title character is assassinated for his ambitiousness. Here are a few lines Brutus speaks: "As he was valiant, I honor him. But as he was ambitious, I slew him." Regardless of whether Brutus intends these lines satirically, as some suggest, Caesar's ruthless willingness to advance himself at the expense of others inspires his assassins to act. This is the ignoble sense of ambition.

There is also a noble sense of ambition: a person who wants to have a positive impact, develop and use skills to the fullest, and benefit the organization. This is the sort of ambition noble leaders demonstrate. In psychology, this is known as the *effectance motive.* Some people are driven to be as effective as they can be in everything they do.

Unless you make it evident you want to lead, you may not be asked to. Part of this willingness ought to be an unwillingness to settle for mediocrity. A desire to lead implies a readiness to take on responsibility. Many people want the benefits that accompany positions of leadership, but they don't want the costs. Demonstrate that you're willing to bear the costs of working harder and staying in your office longer than anyone else.

MAKING THE MOST OF WHAT YOU HAVE

I want briefly to take up the subject of attractiveness, both physical and social, and its relationship to success as a leader. Occasionally, a very attractive woman will fail to get promoted because, through no fault of hers, she makes the men around her uncomfortable. This brings to mind how, occasionally, the most glamorous high school senior may never be asked to the prom because her classmates are intimidated, terrified to ask. This, however, is an exception to the general rule that the world is made for the beautiful people. Although I don't believe this to be literally true—the world was *not* made only or primarily for the beautiful—it is undeniable that physical attractiveness is typically an asset. Good leaders of either gender are routinely well packaged. They dress well, have their hair combed, wear well-polished shoes, and above all have good personal hygiene. Make the most of what you have.

There is also the matter of social attractiveness, which refers to anything, including but not limited to physical appearance, that causes others to want to be around you. In general, the higher you rise in an organization, the more socially attractive you will be. Here are a few other attributes, from among hundreds, that contribute to social attractiveness: walking with self-assurance, being quick and witty, and speaking with a strong but pleasant voice. Again, make the most of what you have.

THE PSYCHOLOGY OF ATTITUDE CHANGE

Leadership often comes down to influence, specifically to changing attitudes, which are predispositions to evaluate or act in specific ways. Perhaps you have an idea, and you want to get others excited about it. Or, you'd like those who report to you to be more careful and stop taking chances. We're once again talking about the art of persuasion.

If your audience is decidedly negative about something, don't flood it with excessively positive statements. Imagine a scale running from –3, through 0, to +3. If your audience is at –2, it's not a good idea to make statements at +3. Doing so will only cause them to become even more negative, to move from –2 to –3. Begin at 0 or +1 and see if you can slowly get them to –1, then to 0, next to +1, and so on. If, to the contrary, your audience is already at +1, by all means start out strong. Try to move them to +2, and eventually to +3.[2]

To be good at moving an audience, whether a single person or a multitude, you have to be able to read that audience's existing attitudes. Machiavelli, however much he may or may not have been a rogue, offered some insightful observations about persuasion.[3] One of them was that it's difficult to lead people counter to their deeply ingrained predispositions. It's therefore rarely a good idea to get too far ahead of those you want to lead, especially if you're trying to persuade them to be more agile, creative, or responsive. Some entrepreneurial leaders are able to move way ahead, to the benefit of their organizations and society. Such occurrences are rare.

Closely related to reading your audience is the need to recognize when a loss is inevitable, and to refrain from expending energy in an effort to prevent it. These are the gravity issues to which we referred in Chapter 12. Reversing the flow of a river is not easy. There may be times when you're going to fail and, in some fashion, suffer a loss, either of prestige or position. You may, for example, be relieved of some if not all of your responsibilities. If this is certain to occur, try to embrace it. To paraphrase notorious San Francisco madam Sally Stanford, "If they're about to run you out of town, get in front of the crowd, and make it look like a parade." Limit your losses.

THE PERSONAL TOUCH

In an article about why some innovations, such as the use of anesthesia, are adopted quickly, while others, like the use of antiseptics, are adopted slowly, surgeon Atul Gawande writes, "Everett Rogers, the great scholar of how new ideas are communicated and spread . . . showed [that] people follow the lead of other people they know and trust." Getting health care professionals on hospital wards to wash their hands, for example, which is still a challenge in many hospitals, is best brought about when they begin to imitate other health care professionals who wash theirs.

Gawande relates how he asked a representative of a pharmaceutical company how he managed to persuade reluctant and "notoriously stubborn" physicians to change drugs. Evidence, replied the rep, was "not even remotely enough." Rather, he applied what he called "the rule of seven touches." By this, he meant he had to make a personal connection, for example by asking the doctor how his daughter's soccer game had gone or personally stocking the doctor's closets with free samples. Only after making such a connection would he ask, "Have you seen this study on our new drug? How about giving it a try?" The rep advised others in his industry, "Personally 'touch' the doctors seven times, and they will come to know you; if they know you, they might trust you; and, if they trust you, they will change."

Unless you're leading a group of volunteers, you may not feel the need to go to all this trouble. But if you want others to internalize your goals, to make them theirs rather than pretending, posturing, or excessively attending to the optics—how they look in your eyes—make the personal connection. "Human interaction," comments Gawande, "is the key force in overcoming resistance and speeding change."[4] To be persuasive, especially over the long haul, you have to achieve more than superficial compliance. You must achieve alignment with your agenda so others help you implement it.

Because of how electronic media has made it quick and easy for people to send messages, handwritten notes are more meaningful than ever. Taking time to write one to someone who's done a good job can mean a great deal; such notes serve as powerful relationship builders. If, however, time gets away from you and it seems too late to handwrite a note, go ahead and send an e-mail or text message, perhaps indicating that you realize your message of appreciation is late. An immediate message of "Good job!" can be wonderfully reinforcing.

Another vehicle for expressing appreciation is the giving of small, inexpensive, but individually well-chosen gifts. A few years ago, I was in

England and noticed in one of the souvenir shops a keychain with the logo of a soccer team I knew a client liked. Although I purchased it out of affection, I realized a year or two later that it created a stronger bond between us. Another way of giving a gift is to forward a magazine article to someone who might have a keen interest in it. Just don't do these sorts of things too often or with too many people because, if you do, it will dilute their effectiveness.

WEAPONS OF PERSUASION

Here are six principles that Robert Cialdini, an expert on social influence, calls *weapons of persuasion:*[5]

1. *Reciprocity:* People tend to return favors. If you help them achieve their objectives, they are more likely to help you achieve yours.
2. *Commitment and consistency:* If you can get others to make a voluntary commitment, they will be reluctant to act in ways contrary to it.
3. *Social proof:* People tend to do what others do, especially if they identify with them and the choices are confusing; we are inclined to imitate others in the decisions we make.
4. *Liking:* Others are more inclined to say *yes*—to do what you want them to do—if they find you attractive, similar to them, and most of all likeable.
5. *Authority:* If other people find you knowledgeable and credible, you are more likely to influence them.
6. *Scarcity:* Many people have a strong drive *not* to lose, so informing them of what they might lose by refusing to say *yes* can be powerful.

This is a pretty good summary of some of the core ingredients that can foster persuasion of any kind.

MINIMIZING REACTANCE

Over the past half-century, social psychologists have noted that people have a strong tendency to react against anyone who tries to control them. When someone attempts to restrict our freedom, we often respond with countercontrol. For this reason, it is wise to give people choices. Consider how much managers may share with their supervisors from 360s. If you leave how much to share up to them, rather than trying to push for self-disclosure, they will tend to disclose more rather than less. Whenever possible, provide options—but not too many because this can backfire by overwhelming people; they begin to agonize about making the *right* decision. Psychologist Barry Schwartz calls this the *paradox of choice*. Giving too many choices sometimes restricts freedom.[6]

The art of persuasion is, in part, maintaining what salespersons call a *yes set*. You want those around you to be naturally inclined toward agreeing with you and your decisions, and the more they've agreed in the past, the more they'll be inclined to agree in the future. It is important, therefore, to avoid, as much as possible, doing anything that triggers a strong negative reaction among your constituents.

This implies that, over the course of your career, you'll have to handle personnel issues with great wisdom. Chapter 8 contains recommendations on what to do, for example, when you have to deal with several underperformers at the same time. The overarching principle is to be thoughtful and methodical in your approach to any challenging personnel problem.

CONSTRUCTIVE SURPRISES

We noted in Chapter 5 how Charles de Gaulle advised leaders always to have a surprise up their sleeves. There is something to this. It's part of entrancing your audience, of remaining an inspiring and persuasive leader. If you're too unpredictable, others will view you as unstable. If, on the other hand, you are entirely predictable, they will see you as boring if not useless, and this is not to the advantage of any leader. Show up when you're least expected. Invite people to your meetings who pleasantly surprise others by their presence. Host little social events that no one expects. The one surprise you should never give them is any kind of public meltdown, which flies in the face of demonstrating stability.

When it comes to surprises, for them to be constructive, you have to maintain the connection between you and your audience, even if that audience is comprised of only a single person. I have seen leaders who, when they spoke with someone, made that person feel like the only human being in the world. It didn't matter who was waiting, even a VIP a few feet away. Their focus remained fixed on the other person.

I have also seen leaders who do not do this and therefore pay a price in terms of their ability to influence others. When they're talking with someone, instead of moving *into* the conversation, they move *out of* it, by actively scanning the environment for whoever else might want to talk to them, or whatever else might be going on. Their attention shifts rapidly from person to person and group to group. Make eye contact and keep making it, and unless a fire alarm goes off, make the other person feel singularly special.

THE POTENTIAL VALUE OF PRATFALLS

I also want to take up the subject of pratfalls and how they can help or hurt, depending on the status of the leader. A pratfall is an embarrassing blunder, like spilling a glass of wine on the table at a formal banquet, getting up to the podium and noticing some part of your clothing is unfastened, or falling into the water at a dockside party. If you're an ordinary person and one of these things happens, others may be inclined to raise their eyebrows.

If, by contrast, you're a person the group looks up to, such a mishap may endear you to them. Sometimes, therefore, it's a good idea, if you're with people who may be intimidated by your position in the organization, to appear a little less than perfect now and then. If you spill your coffee, crack a joke at your own expense. Others will bond to you more if they see you as human.

MAKE IT FUN

There is little that is more effective for increasing your persuasive power than, as much as possible, making work fun. Dwight D. Eisenhower remarked, "Leadership is the art of getting someone else to do something you want done because he wants to do it." Charismatic leaders often have the ability to turn toilsome work into joyful play.

Alluding to how, by portraying the painting of a fence as play, Tom talked his friends into painting it, psychologists began to talk about the *Tom Sawyer effect*. Although we can't all be equally charismatic, we can at least move in that direction by injecting a bit of playfulness into what otherwise might be drudgery.

There is nothing quite like the camaraderie that emerges from tackling a seemingly impossible task and completing it successfully, provided you foster a we're-in-this-together mentality and occasionally take breaks for enjoyable bonding activities. These can range from bringing in donuts or pizza, to taking your team out for dinner.

PERSUASIVE COLLABORATION

You will never advance as far as you otherwise could if you lack the capacity to collaborate, particularly as a member of a group. This implies that you have the ability to "play well with others"—to function effec-tively as a member of a team—and hinges directly on your ability to be persuasive. Persuasiveness is wonderful insurance against becoming frus-trated with colleagues.

Persuasively collaborating is pivotally linked to our discussion in Chapter 8 relating to flexible assertiveness. There's a time to lead and a time to follow. It's also related to your mastery of the attributes dis-cussed in the previous four chapters—insight, restraint, nobility, and compassion.

Teamwork is a critically important skill. If you don't acquire it, you'll define yourself as an individual contributor, which will often limit your opportunities for promotion.

PERSUASIVE COMMUNICATION

Persuasive leaders speak the language of their constituents. If, for example, a leader has an advanced degree in English and knows lots of five-syllable words, that leader would not be well advised to use many of them with groups that might roll their eyes. The savvy leader will keep the presentation straightforward, using words and phrases familiar to the audience. When an effective leader is talking one-on-one with someone, especially a person the leader wants to persuade, the leader may, without realizing it, instinctively mirror the pace of the other person's speech. If he or she talks fast, so will the leader. If the person talks slowly, the leader will also.

It's important to be able to stand in front of a group and effectively promote your ideas. If you have to make an important presentation, the best thing you can do is thoroughly prepare. Overlearn what you're going to say. Rehearse it again and again, until you've so mastered the content that you're sick of it. To enhance naturalness and connect with your audi-ence, use an outline rather than a word-for-word script, although for an audience of more than a hundred or so, a script may work nicely. If you use a script, practice until you can deliver your material with appropri-ate dramatic emphasis, and without looking as if you're reading. Record your talk and play it back. Do this over and over. Time your presentation, so that you can be reasonably sure of staying within the prescribed lim-its. If you use visual aids, don't march through them word-by-word. Use them for their intended purposes, as *aids*. Be assertive when you speak, so that you project confidence and expertise. Sometimes it's good to practice dropping the pitch of your voice a bit, since under pressure a speaker's pitch tends to rise.

NEGOTIATING SKILL

Your effectiveness, in the long run, has a lot to do with your skill at negotiation. This skill is directly related to knowing how to be persuasive. Not that this will always get you everything you want, but it will at least enable you to get a good deal of it.

You can't work long in any organization without having to negotiate. What you negotiate can range from the use of a room to working out the compensation package for someone you want to hire, promote, or retain. Whatever the subject, there is considerable merit in learning how to do this in a way that minimizes hard feelings, both in you and the other person. Harvard still runs workshops on effective negotiation, the content for which derives from what has come to be known as the Harvard Negotiation Project. A convenient way to learn some of its key principles is to read Fisher and Ury's 1983 *Getting to Yes: Negotiating Agreement Without Giving In.* I have taught these principles and personally used them. They work.

The essence of what the book recommends is to negotiate from deeper interests rather than fixed positions and, whenever possible, to appeal to an external standard. To illustrate how you might negotiate from interests, let's return to the example we used in Chapter 8, where we discussed the potential value of negative timing. Imagine once again that you chair a board equally divided over changing the name of a nonprofit organization. Both sides begin from a fixed position, either *yes,* change it, or *no,* don't. If you explore further, however, you might discover that those who don't want to change the name are principally concerned that such a change would dishonor the founder, while those who want to change it are primarily concerned that the name more clearly communicate its purpose. There might be a way to continue to honor the founder while also better conveying the mission of the organization.

To illustrate how external standards can help, suppose you were about to make an offer on a house. The first thing you or your real estate agent might do is look up the *comps* for houses about the same size, with roughly the same amenities, in the same neighborhood. You'd want to know at what price they are currently listed or have recently been sold. Another example is a human resources department using a salary survey to determine how much to offer a person who is being recruited into a job. As with the real estate transaction, they want to know the market.

ASKING AND LISTENING

We have already touched on the Socratic method. To review, asking well-framed questions is among the best ways to gather information. That much is obvious. What may not be obvious is that you can use this method to persuade, to lead. By asking carefully crafted questions in a neutral tone of voice, you may be able to put others in the position of having to justify what they want to do. This is especially helpful if what they're advocating makes no sense. It's also helpful for leading others to what you consider to be the right conclusion or best course. Once you frame the question, the answer is potentially at hand.

We've also taken note of how important it is to listen and to make sure you hear what's being said. I learned a long time ago that most CEOs are good listeners. They know more about what's going on in their organizations than you might expect. Keep in mind, as you listen, there are no jokes. This, of course, is not literally true, but it makes a good point. When people make critical or disparaging comments and then try to water them down with "I was only kidding," the odds are they weren't. Such utterances convey more than a grain of truth about what these people think.

Wise leaders do not allow themselves to be put in the position of believing they've convinced others, only to find out later there was a misunderstanding. It is often helpful, therefore, to write a confirmatory e-mail message, stating what your understanding is, and asking for a response. This allows you to create a written record of what you collectively agreed to.

TRIBAL RITUALS

You will be more persuasive if those around you view you as loyal to the tribe. Many years ago, I realized that organizations were, by and large, tribes, not families, and I'm not the only person to have reached this conclusion. Some organizations are more familial than others, but at root they all remain tribes. Unless you have done something heinous, your family will take you in. You may have to go to the back door, but a way will nearly always be found to provide you with a meal and a place to sleep. A tribe, by contrast, will sacrifice its members for the good of the tribe.

Although you may have a few real friends at work, the vast majority of your relationships with co-workers are instrumental—transactional. You and they interact because both of you serve the enterprise—the tribe—not because of affectional bonds. People who do not reckon with this can have a rude awakening when they retire. No one calls. Or, at least relatively few former co-workers do.

It's prudent to attend certain functions because they are important *tribal rituals*. On top of that, they may be enjoyable. But, such events remain quasi-business meetings—no matter how casual they appear. We've already noted why it's important to keep in mind that leaders are always *on*. Never attend a social function with others from your organization and forget that you're being observed. Everything you do is, in some sense, on the record.

IDIOSYNCRASY CREDITS

To the extent that you further the goals of an organization, you build up an invisible bank account of what Edwin Hollander long ago labeled idiosyncrasy credits. You can also think of these as persuasion points, which you can spend to compensate for violating its norms or perhaps even breaking its rules. If, for example, you've won a Nobel Prize and are on the faculty of many universities, you will enjoy an almost unlimited number of them. Therefore, if you fail to show up for your office hours or miss a class you're scheduled to teach, the worst that may happen is that the provost, its chief academic officer, will stop by and deferentially ask you to meet, at least now and then, with the post-docs. Because they want to keep you and publicize your presence, you have the license, within reason, to do almost anything you want.

Over the span of your career, you will accumulate a certain number of these sorts of credits. But you will never know exactly how many you have. It is important not to overspend your account, because if you do, you'll be branded as a user, opportunist, or worse. Just as you will never know for sure how large your account is, you may never perceive that you've been so branded. Be sure you maintain a healthy balance.

THE SECRET OF POWERFULLY PERSUASIVE LEADERSHIP

Highly persuasive leaders are able to move others into something that, at times, resembles a trance. Life is filled with trancelike moments, only we usually don't think of them that way. Such moments, long or short, blend smoothly into our ongoing mental life. We noted near the end of the last chapter how even watching a good movie can put us into a kind of trance. So can many other common experiences, like listening to music or becoming engrossed in a book.

Here's what a trancelike state is and is not. In such a state, we do not fall asleep or become drowsy, and if we do, the trancelike state evaporates. We remain alert, attentive, and often but not always tranquil. During trancelike moments, we decrease our peripheral awareness and become absorbed in whatever or whoever is entrancing us, and so we narrow our mental focus.

In our ordinary waking moments, we continually scan our environments for danger. Living as we do in a relatively well-ordered society, we are largely protected from serious threats. No one is likely to show up at our door brandishing a machine gun. Marines fly overhead, missile-armed carriers and submarines roam the oceans, and we have large, well-trained, and well-equipped land forces. We also have the National Guard and enjoy the stabilizing effects of local, state, and national law enforcement agencies. So, unless we live in a high-crime area, we rarely if ever have to scan our surroundings for lethal danger. But we still subconsciously scan, even if we're relaxing on the sofa. Doing this has been bred into us over a very long time. The vigilant survived and lived to pass on their genes; the non-vigilant didn't.

When we're in a trancelike state, scanning either stops or is markedly reduced, which is why it can be so jarring for someone behind us in a movie theater to kick our seat.[7] Being in a trancelike state is like trading in a shotgun for a rifle. We no longer cover the whole field but, instead, attend to a small region of it more intently. This is the sort of thing that happens when we become enrolled and enfranchised, when we accept someone as a leader. To a greater or lesser extent, we suspend our environmental scanning, in the belief that the leader will look out for our interests. The more we trust the leader, the more this is so.

Allowing someone to entrance you can be a mistake, since this makes it more likely that you will disregard or miss important data. Failing to turn data into information or see their implications is the potential price of surrendering vigilance. If the person you're surrendering it to is a scoundrel, you are at risk. Think of the financial devastation inflicted on trusting investors by unscrupulous investment fund managers.

Some extraordinarily persuasive leaders are so diabolical that they become genocidal. Adolf Hitler enchanted—entranced—much of the German populace during the 1930s, in the increasingly sinister run-up to World War II. In many cases, the trance lasted well into the 1940s, long after it was obvious to any rational person that Germany had lost the war.

Genocidal goals are the earmark of the deranged, but this, unfortunately, does not make them ineffective leaders, whether in the political or financial arena. Their capacity to enroll and enfranchise others serves as a key enabler of their perversity. If Adolf Hitler, Joseph Stalin, Idi Amin, Pol Pot, and others had used their persuasive powers for good, imagine the countless lives that could have been enriched rather than ended, and the senseless wars that could have been averted. Regardless of their aims, whether noble or nefarious, all famous or infamous leaders are persuasive.

CONCLUDING COMMENTS

The core of persuasiveness is interpersonal skill, and you can't develop this unless you spend time with people. No one learns to be an effective leader by acquiring an MBA. We learn by making a hundred decisions every month and a thousand every year, and sometimes banging our heads against the wall for being so stupid. The only kind of training that works is OTJ—on the job.

People learn to be leaders by getting nicked, taking note of the blood on their shirts, and learning how better to thrust and parry. Learning to be a leader is like learning to play tennis. You have to spend a lot of time hitting the ball. To play well takes many hours of practice, some natural talent, and a love for the game.

I wish you great success as you develop and refine your approaches to building trust and connecting with people. Remember, everyone makes mistakes. The trick is to forgive yourself, learn from your mistakes, and persevere.

SIXTEEN

The Big Five, Interpersonal Effectiveness, and Leadership Development

In the preceding chapters, we have discussed ten traits and their associated strategies for building trust. These are the best ones I know. It would not be fitting to end this book, however, without revisiting two questions. The first has to do with how the two sets of five relate to each other, and the second concerns how easy or difficult it is to develop any one of them.

INTERCONNECTIONS BETWEEN AND AMONG THE STRATEGIES

Imagine, for a moment, that each of the strategies in Part II is made of a different alloy. Alloys are combinations of two or more metals. Brass, for example, is composed of copper and zinc, both of which are more or less pure metals. Pewter is mostly tin mixed either with copper, antimony, bismuth, lead, or silver. Bronze is primarily copper with a bit of tin thrown in. So, we might reasonably ask, which strategies are the pure metals and which ones the alloys? How, in other words, do the two sets of five relate to each other?

We know that all ten are important, but as I have noted, the relationship between the two sets of five is not well understood. Based on over a half-century of research, I have suggested that the first set, the Big Five, are the pure metals—the source traits—while the second set relating to interpersonal effectiveness (IE) are the alloys.

If so, for each one in the second set, we may ask which of the five pure metals go into making it, and in what proportions? It seems probable, for example, that nobility, one facet of IE, is directly related to conscientiousness, a dimension of the Big Five. It might also relate to stability and friendliness, two other Big Five dimensions. But the question remains, how much of each of these three components go into making a person behave selflessly as opposed to treacherously?

When we come to some other facets of IE, it is difficult to come up with hypotheses that get us even this far. How, for example, might we use the Big Five to explain persuasiveness? We can make educated guesses, but as in our attempt to explain selflessness, they would remain just that. We are left with the statement that graduate students in behavioral science learn to end exam papers with: "More research is needed."

Yet, I again want to emphasize that there is no question that all ten strategies are important for fostering trust and therefore to leadership. Nor is these any serious doubt about the Big Five being foundational.

CAN THE STRATEGIES BE LEARNED?

Yes, they can be. Management professor Warren Bennis remarked, "The most dangerous leadership myth is that leaders are born—that there is a genetic factor to leadership . . . in fact the opposite is true. Leaders are made rather than born." As suggested throughout this book, sustained practice is essential, but it does pay off. Changing the wellsprings—the Big Five source traits outlined in Part I—requires patience and persistence. So does changing the five facets of IE discussed in Part II.

Let's return briefly to intellect, the trait that seems most resistant to change. Are you likely through practice to become better at conceptual thinking, cogent analysis, and intuitive reasoning? If you frame the question in terms of becoming a second Einstein, it can lead you to the cynical quip: "You can't get out what God didn't put in." If, however, you frame the question in terms of maximizing the capabilities you already have, I believe you will come to an altogether different conclusion. The same line of reasoning applies to the other nine attributes.

Too many people assume it can't be done. Within broad limits, *it can be done,* as long as you keep at it. Can the strategies be learned? You bet they can. They absolutely can.

Appendix

If you ever decide to see a therapist or a counselor, it's important to find a good one, someone with the relevant education, experience, and emotional well-being—and, someone with whom you feel comfortable and enjoy good interpersonal chemistry. This could be a psychologist, a psychiatrist, a social worker, a marriage and family therapist, or a member of the clergy.

Provided a surgeon is not seriously disturbed, the surgeon's mental status may not much affect a surgical outcome. The personality and mental well-being of a psychological professional, however, can make a great deal of difference. A therapist's principal tool is his or her *person,* which has implications for maturity and wisdom. Except under certain employment arrangements, a person must be licensed in most if not all states to use the title of physician, psychologist, marriage and family therapist, or clinical social worker. This, however, is generally not true of the general term counselor. Unfortunately, even holding a license is, of itself, no certification of sound mental health or good judgment.

Another difficulty is that in many states physicians' and psychologists' licenses are generic. A physician can claim to be, and function as, a neurologist, psychiatrist, dermatologist, surgeon, you name it; similarly, there are at least eleven or twelve specialties within psychology (educational, physiological, social, etc.), only a few of which require clinical training. Licensing boards exhort licensees to practice within the limits of their qualifications, and if they don't, they are more likely to be censured or sued, but this doesn't always happen. Both social workers and marriage/family therapists are similarly encouraged to work within the limits of their training and experience.

Physicians often have to be granted hospital privileges, which are becoming increasingly difficult to obtain without board certification in a specialty; it is usually safe, therefore, to assume that a doctor who claims to be a psychiatrist has, in fact, been trained as one, especially if he or she is practicing in an urban area. Since most nonpsychiatric mental health practitioners do not need hospital privileges, it's easier for any who have not been adequately trained to gloss over this, which is why it's important to get as much specific information about a practitioner as you can. You can often obtain useful information from your state's online registries.

Make a list of two or three practitioners you would like to try. The best way to develop such a list is to inquire—ask around. Ask your primary care physician, clergyperson, and perhaps anyone with whom you have rapport and know has consulted a mental health practitioner. Then, make an appointment with each one. Seeing several will take more time and cost more money, but choosing the wrong practitioner can prove far more costly in the long run. Not every professional is right for every client. See them all once, and then, without burning any bridges, select one to see for a month. If, at the end of a month, you don't both believe the visits are productive, try one of the others. Keep in mind that you do not have to continue seeing anyone you don't want to see. You are the final judge of whether or not the sessions are doing you any good. If you work for a company with an employee assistance program (EAP), that might be a good place to start.

Many people worry that, if they see a therapist, they will be stigmatized. If you use insurance to help pay for your visits, the practitioner will probably have to submit a diagnosis to your insurance provider. Wary of this, a small percentage of people prefer to pay these expenses out of pocket. The important thing is to get whatever assistance you need.

Notes

CHAPTER 1

1. William J. Reddin, *Managerial Effectiveness* (New York: McGraw-Hill, 1970).

2. Paul Hersey, Kenneth H. Blanchard, and Dewey E. Johnson, *Management of Organizational Behavior: Leading Human Resources* (Upper Saddle River, NJ: Prentice Hall, 2012). First published in 1969, now in its 10th edition.

3. Victor H. Vroom and Philip W. Yetton, *Leadership and Decision-Making* (Pittsburgh: University of Pittsburgh Press, 1973).

4. Peter Salovey and John D. Mayer, "Emotional Intelligence," *Imagination, Cognition, and Personality* 9 (1990): 185–211.

5. Daniel Goleman, *Emotional Intelligence* (New York: Bantam Books, 1995).

CHAPTER 2

1. Colin L. Powell with Joseph E. Persico, *My American Journey* (New York: Random House, 1995): 50.

CHAPTER 3

1. Stephen J. Zaccaro, "Trait-Based Perspectives of Leadership," *American Psychologist* 62 (2007): 6–16.

2. Five, if you subsume creativity under intellect, which is what most researchers believe is correct.

3. Begin with the first source trait, intellect. We have three options (high, medium, low). Similarly, we also have three options for rating the second source trait, stability. So, considering only the first two source traits, and disregarding the other three for now, we can generate 3 × 3 or 9 profiles (see Chapter 9 for examples). Now, for each of the nine profiles we already have, construct three new ones by adding either high, medium, or low on the third source trait, conscientiousness. This gives us 9 × 3 or 27 profiles, and we haven't yet considered the last two of the five wellsprings. Remember that, for each of the source traits, you can give three possible ratings. Whether you rate a person on any one of the five as high, medium, or low has nothing to do with how you rate that person on the other four.

CHAPTER 4

1. David Wechsler, *WAIS-IV: Technical and Interpretive Manual,* 4th ed. (San Antonio: Pearson, 2008), 3.

2. It is now believed that such people are not so much intellectually deficient as autistic.

3. Daniel Kahneman, *Thinking Fast and Slow* (New York: Farrar, Strauss and Giroux, 2011).

4. This statement has been attributed to Abraham Lincoln.

CHAPTER 5

1. The title of the poem is simply *If.*

2. Laurence J. Peter and Raymond Hull, *The Peter Principle: Why Things Always Go Wrong* (New York: William Morrow and Company, 1969).

3. Clinton W. McLemore and David W. Brokaw, "Personality Disorders as Dysfunctional Interpersonal Behavior," *Journal of Personality Disorders* 1(3) (1987): 270–285.

4. Manfred F. R. Kets de Vries and Danny Miller, *Unstable at the Top: Inside the Troubled Organization* (New York: New American Library, 1988).

CHAPTER 7

1. Note the spelling of *complement,* with an *e* not an *i.* Complement, here, means to do the opposite.

2. Robert K. Greenleaf, *The Servant as Leader* (Westfield, IN: The Robert K. Greenleaf Center for Servant Leadership, 1991).

3. Behaviors put on what psychologists call a *partial reinforcement schedule* can be extremely resistant to extinction.

4. The price of criticism is a better idea, and I can't remember him ever having come up with one.

CHAPTER 8

1. Many professions have subtle code words or phrases that can be used in a pejorative way. For those in management, one of these is "not a team player." Although such a description may be appropriate as a way of characterizing a particular person, other times it's just a way to slam someone with different opinions.

2. My all-time favorite Chinese proverb is, "The wise man can play the fool, but the fool can't play the wise man." It has many parallels. A great thinker, for example, may be a poor writer, but a good writer cannot be a poor thinker. One's ability to think sets an upper limit to how well one can write.

3. John Keegan, *The Mask of Command* (New York: Viking, 1987).

CHAPTER 10

1. The best succinct discussion of how emotional intelligence relates to leadership is the 1998 article by Daniel Goleman, "What Makes a Leader?" published in *Harvard Business Review* (reprint # 98606). I have ordered reprints of it that I've given to hundreds of clients and have also had them ordered for conferences I've facilitated. See also Daniel Goleman, *Emotional Intelligence* (New York: Bantam Books, 1995).

2. For purposes of our discussion, I am bypassing discussion of the relatively new concept of epigenesis.

3. The dimensions of the Big Five are not hidden; unlike genes, you can observe them, or at least infer their existence, without special equipment. Yet, thinking of the Big Five as a person's genotype and of IE as part of that person's phenotype may be helpful.

4. Face validity refers to the appearance of something as a robust predictor, which psychologists discovered over a century ago may or may not be the case.

5. Human behavior is not easy to explain, in part because people can always exercise their freedom of choice to defy prediction.

CHAPTER 11

1. This, of course, is the title of a Eugene O'Neill play.

2. "Do you want to invest $20,000 in this product or that one?" involves the assumption that you want to invest in one of them. You may not want to invest in either. Unwarranted assumptions are sometimes called *suppressed premises*.

3. He was a walking Márquez novel in which a single sentence runs on for pages, which is what occurs in his 1975 *Autumn of the Patriarch*.

4. There is some sense to this since anxiety and depression often go hand in hand. Nevertheless, the blanket cross-marketing of an antidepressant to treat anxiety can be a stretch.

5. See the related material in Chapter 8 concerning gentle unrelenting pressure; keep in mind that *gentle* sometimes has to be operationalized as *not too often*.

6. There are essential differences between good and bad chiefs. Good chiefs have the vision to see where their tribes or subtribes need to go, often before anyone else has much of an inkling, and the capacity to lead them there. Bad chiefs, by contrast, lack vision, capacity, or both. They talk the language of the tribe but are myopically preoccupied with their own outcomes, which leaves them with little time or energy to think deeply about the welfare of the tribe.

7. "Cover your ass" behavior.

8. These come from RDI's Leadership Effectiveness Survey (LES).

9. These are intended to be gender-neutral terms.

CHAPTER 12

1. I knew one manager who was so skilled at transcending the leader's dilemma that he could fire someone and then have the person thank him for it.

CHAPTER 13

1. Quoted in Adam Grant, "In the Company of Givers and Takers," *Harvard Business Review* (April 2013): 97. See also Adam Grant, "Givers Take All: The Hidden Dimension of Corporate Culture," *McKinsey Quarterly* (April 2013), and Adam Grant, *Give and Take: A Revolutionary Approach to Success* (New York: Viking, 2013).

2. These workshops are based on my *Street-Smart Ethics: Succeeding in Business without Selling Your Soul* (Louisville: Westminster John Knox Press, 2003).

3. Ryan Lizza, "Leading from Behind," *The New Yorker,* April 27, 2011.

4. Words not only communicate ideas. They also shape them and summon us to honor their implications and nuances. Hence, word choice is not trivial.

5. Unfortunately, that is how many corporate leaders are often incented by their boards.

CHAPTER 14

1. *The American Heritage College Dictionary,* 3rd ed. (Boston: Houghton Mifflin Company, 1993).

2. *The American Heritage College Dictionary.*

3. *The American Heritage College Dictionary.*

4. First published in 1923 as *Ich und Dich,* it was later translated into English as *I and Thou.*

5. Notice the counterproductive use of *always* and *never* in each of the three complaints.

6. William Ickes, "Empathic Accuracy," *Journal of Personality* 61(4) (1993): 587–610.

7. By *good* novel, I mean something other than the usual action or spy story, although even some of these can prove helpful in augmenting empathic capacity.

CHAPTER 15

1. See James C. Collins and Jerry I. Porras, "Building Your Company's Vision," *Harvard Business Review* (September–October 1996). Reprint # 96501. This article became a chapter in the revised edition of *Built to Last: Successful Habits of Visionary Companies* (New York: HarperCollins, 1994).

2. These recommendations are based on Osgood and Tannenbaum's *congruity theory.*

3. Machiavelli was not so much prescribing ethical norms as depicting political realities, at least as he observed them in and around Renaissance Florence.

4. Atul Gawande, "Slow Ideas," *The New Yorker* (July 29, 2013): 36–45.

5. Robert B. Cialdini, *Influence: Science and Practice,* 5th ed. (Boston: Allyn and Bacon, 2008).

6. Barry Schwartz, *The Paradox of Choice: Why More Is Less* (New York: Ecco, 2004).

7. In some trancelike states, awareness of everything in one's environment, for example every sound, is substantially heightened.

Index

About the Author

Clinton W. McLemore holds a PhD in psychology from the University of Southern California. Both a clinical and organizational psychologist, he is president and CEO of Relational Dynamics, Inc. (RDI). For fifteen years, he was a full-time professor and, for nine of these, taught in a doctoral clinical psychology program. Dr. McLemore's articles have been published in many professional journals, including the *American Psychologist,* one of whose reviewers described his work as a "seminal contribution to the field." He has written many invited book chapters and six previous books, including *Street-Smart Ethics: Succeeding in Business without Selling Your Soul* (Westminster John Knox, 2003).

In 1980, he founded Relational Dynamics, Inc. (RDI) and has consulted for many Fortune 500 companies. He has appeared on numerous radio and television shows and his ideas about behavior change have been written about in such publications as *Harvard Business Review, Securities Industry Daily,* and *Today's Leader.* Dr. McLemore also founded *Clinician's Research Digest,* which was used as a prop in the film *Good Will Hunting.* The *Digest* is now owned and operated by the American Psychological Association.

CPSIA information can be obtained
at www.ICGtesting.com
Printed in the USA
LVOW04*1937030616

491119LV00015B/162/P

JUN -- 2016